D1642468

TOWNLEY GRAMMAR SCHOOL

R03365F0566

Townley Grammar School for Girls

20954

796

Visions of Sport

Visions of Sport

A CELEBRATION OF THE WORK OF
THE ALLSPORT PHOTOGRAPHIC AGENCY.
THE WORLD'S FINEST
SPORTS PHOTOGRAPHY.

KENSINGTON WEST
PRODUCTIONS

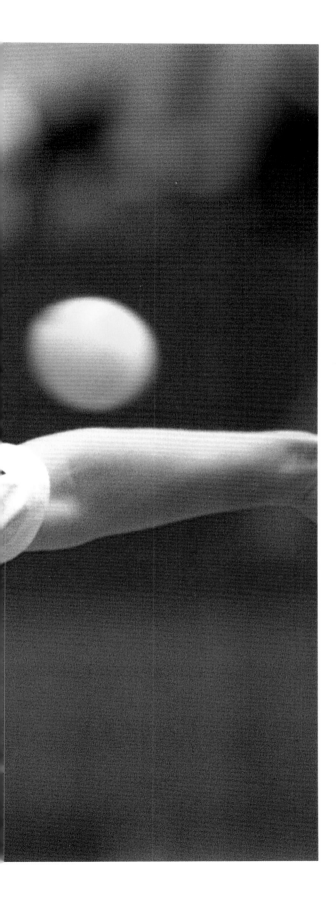

First published in 1993 by
Kensington West Productions Ltd
5 Cattle Market, Hexham
Northumberland NE46 1NJ

A CIP catalogue record for this book is available from the British Library

ISBN 18713449932X

Picture Editor: Bob Martin
Picture Researcher (UK): Tony Hicks
Picture Researcher (US): Stephanie Mullen
Editorial Contributors: Nick Edmund and Peter Nichols

Designed by Rob Kelland at Allsport

Origination by Ashford Scanning, England
Printed in Italy by New Interlitho S.p.A.

Canon is the registered trademark of Canon Inc.

All rights reserved. No part of this publication may be reproduced,
stored in a retrieval system, or transmitted in any form or by any
means, electronic, mechanical, photocopying, recording or otherwise,
without the prior permission of Kensington West Productions Ltd.
While every effort has been made to ensure the accuracy of
the facts and data contained in this publication, no responsibility
can be accepted by Allsport, or Kensington West Productions Ltd,
for errors or omissions or their consequences.

© 1993 Allsport Photographic

Ballesteros and Olazabal at the 18th (half-title page)
PHOTOGRAPH BY CHRIS COLE

Olympic flame (frontispiece)
PHOTOGRAPH BY DAVID CANNON

Diving Shadow (title page)
PHOTOGRAPH BY SIMON BRUTY

Jana Novotna (left)
PHOTOGRAPH BY SIMON BRUTY

INTRODUCTION

TWENTY-FIVE YEARS as a leading light in the sports photographic industry is cause for celebration – hence this book *Visions of Sport* which brings together some of the best work of the photographers of the Allsport agency.

Visions of Sport contains over 140 photographs from a variety of sports and events around the world and gives just a glimpse of the originality and depth of what is internationally recognised as the biggest and best sports picture archive. This archive is based in London and Los Angeles with over six million pictures now on file, including many which are stored digitally.

This is in fact the second *Visions of Sport*. The first, published five years ago, contained many excellent photographs, but since that time, the range and quality of pictures taken has been such that our twenty-fifth anniversary presented us with a golden opportunity to produce another book, one which I feel is the equal of anything in its field.

All pictures in this book are new, except the black and white photograph which immortalised the American long-jumper, Bob Beamon. This picture, taken in 1968 by Tony Duffy, now a highly respected professional, but at that time just a hopeful amateur pursuing his hobby, was the starting point of the agency and a touchstone whereby we are able to judge the qualities of sports photography.

The Beamon picture says it all; the grace, the power, the skill, the effort – but why use words, the full gamut of expressions is captured in this photograph and those that follow on the proceeding pages. Now of course the pictures are in colour, the level of technique, due to innovations such as the Canon EOS system, has improved dramatically and yet these pictures are still about the level of commitment of people. This commitment has been made most ostensibly by the subjects of the photographs, but it has also been made by the photographers themselves, and *Visions of Sport* is a tribute to them all.

In the same way that the outstanding contributors of articles are all winners in their chosen sporting pursuit, so too are the Allsport photographers who between them have won over 100 national and international awards for excellence.

The image of Bob Beamon shattering the world record in Mexico has always been synonymous with Allsport – but things change and all records are there to be broken. So in 1991 when photographer Mike Powell captured the image of another American long-jumper, his namesake Mike Powell breaking that record in Tokyo, how fitting it was that he came from the Allsport agency.

Visions of Sport, like many of the photographs included in it, would not have been possible without the support of Canon. Canon Europa, too, is celebrating its 25th birthday and Allsport is proud to be associated with this company and its products. They also have my personal respect and admiration for their friendly and professional support of sports photographers worldwide, regardless of camera system used. This commitment to service and innovation is reflected in this book through the use of the Canon EOS System, probably the most important breakthrough in camera technology in the last twenty five years.

STEVE POWELL

PHOTOGRAPHER

GROUP MANAGING DIRECTOR
ALLSPORT PHOTOGRAPHIC

Diver Tracey Miles is captured high over the Sagrada Familia in Barcelona.

Tracey Miles diving over Barcelona
PHOTOGRAPH BY BOB MARTIN

*M*id-air acrobatics are the domain of the pole vaulter and foot
volleyball player alike.

Houston pole vault (above)
PHOTOGRAPH BY TIM DEFRISCO

Sepak Takraw (right)
PHOTOGRAPH BY MIKE POWELL

*F*rench 90 metre ski jumper, Francis Repellin, appears
to be frozen in mid flight while the EUN Four Man
Bobsled team suffer the additional hazard of having
a crew member seated facing the wrong way!

Francis Repellin (left)
PHOTOGRAPH BY SHAUN BOTTERILL

EUN Four Man Bobsled Team (above)
PHOTOGRAPH BY SIMON BRUTY

Finn Jagge of Norway throws up a powder snow scene during a Men's Slalom race at Madonna di Campiglio, Italy.

Finn Jagge at Madonna
PHOTOGRAPH BY SIMON BRUTY

A frozen lake provides unconventional ground for horse racing at St Moritz.

Horse Racing On Ice

PHOTOGRAPH BY BOB MARTIN

Whatever the nature of the terrain, somehow, it seems, man will find a way of racing a motor cycle across it. Ice and sand provide interesting topographic challenges to the speedway riders at Frankfurt and the scramblers at Le Touquet.

Ice Speedway (above)
PHOTOGRAPH BY BOB MARTIN

Scrambling at Le Touquet (right)
PHOTOGRAPH BY BOB MARTIN

A lone rider in the 1990
Super Bikes contest at
Donington is trapped in
the last of the evening
sunlight.

Lone Super Bike Rider
Photograph by Chris Cole

"AND FROM DESPAIR
THUS HIGH UPLIFTED BEYOND HOPE"

MILTON, PARADISE LOST, 1608 – 1674

MIKE POWELL

I STILL LOOK BACK at the tape of that competition. Not so much to remind myself of what I achieved, but how I achieved it. I look at it from a technical standpoint, of course. I look at speed and lift and extension and things like that, but I also look at it for motivation. That day in Tokyo, when I took Beamon's record, I was in such a focused state of mind, I felt so positive and had such conviction that this was my day. That helped so much, was so important.

Man, it's hard to explain exactly how I felt. I had been trying to earn my own name for a long time. Carl had all the attention in the event and I was living in the shadow. Yet I knew before the World Championships that he could be beaten. I had come within one centimetre in the US trials and I felt sure of my abilities on the day. The people close to me understood. They knew how hard I had been working and they saw the conviction on my face when I told them. I wasn't overconfident, but I knew that I was better.

When I saw the mark 8.95m go up, I realised straight off exactly what I had achieved. I didn't need time for it to sink in. Carl, I believe, was in shock. He had been number one for a long time and he wasn't the only one who thought that when the record finally went, it would be him that did it.

When you achieve something like that you have to re-evaluate your goals. You can't break the world record every time you go out and jump, so there's no sense in trying to do that. Instead, you have to set yourself other challenges. Ones that are attainable.

I feel I have to be improving all the time, so I have concentrated on the quality of my average performance. In 1991, when I broke the record I was averaging around 8.43m for each winning jump. Last summer, although I only competed about eight times, I took that up to around 8.50m. This summer, my objective is to ease the plateau still higher.

Track is very satisfying like that. It gives you very practical goals. It's not like anything else. If you wanted to be the best sportswriter or the best photographer in the world that's hard, because we all have different ideas of what is an exceptional piece of writing or what the perfect picture is. How do you measure it?

Track is beautiful because it allows you to make these objective measurements. Your goals can be very precise. You know that if you put the work in, then you can register those achievements. The goals are real and practical. I enjoy that. I have to. I live with, eat with and sleep with Track every day of my life.

MIKE POWELL

STUTTGART · AUGUST 1993

Mike Powell at the 1992 Olympics, Barcelona
PHOTOGRAPH BY MIKE POWELL

'V' is for victory as
Andre Philips savours the
occasion after defeating
the great Ed Moses.
Philips won his gold in the
400 metre hurdles at
Seoul in 1988. An equally
glorious moment for Colin
Jackson as he triumphs in
the 110 metre hurdles
and sets a new world
record in the 1993
World Championships
at Stuttgart.

Andre Philips (left)
PHOTOGRAPH BY CHRIS COLE

Colin Jackson (right)
PHOTOGRAPH BY GRAY MORTIMORE

*T*he emotional mix. The picture of despair and defeat rarely
changes but feelings of joy and victory can produce the full range
of expressions as evidenced by these British rowers, winners of the
Gold Medal for the coxed pairs at the 1992 Barcelona Olympics

The Searle brothers and Garry Herbert (above)
PHOTOGRAPH BY MIKE POWELL

Dejected Cuban Wrestler (right)
PHOTOGRAPH BY MIKE POWELL

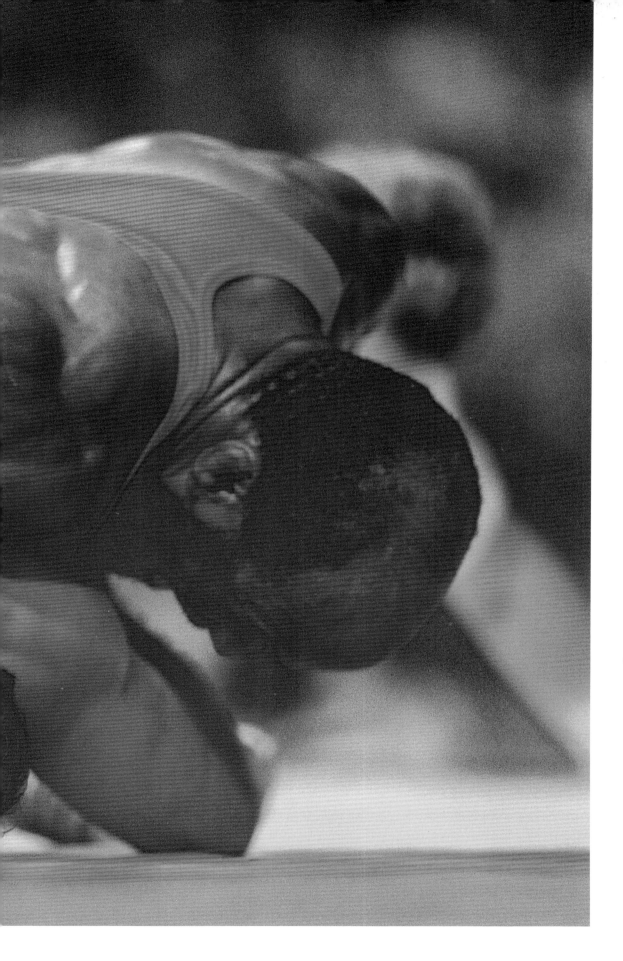

American Chris Campbell appears to be crushing the very lifeblood out of New Zealander Terrence Parker in the 90kg Greco-Roman Wrestling event at the Barcelona Olympic Games.

Greco-Roman Wrestling

PHOTOGRAPH BY SHAUN BOTTERILL

*E*xcruciating pain for an injured German hockey player at the
Barcelona Olympics. Sheer joy and jubilation for swimmer
Adrian Moorhouse after winning the Final of the 100 metres
Breaststroke at Seoul in 1988.

Injured hockey player (above)
PHOTOGRAPH BY CHRIS COLE

Adrian Moorhouse (right)
PHOTOGRAPH BY TONY DUFFY

*F*ew in the footballing world have displayed or generated as much passion and emotion as Paul Gascoigne and Brian Clough: the former is pictured following England's defeat by West Germany in the semi-finals of the World Cup and the latter during his final days as Manager of Nottingham Forest.

Gazza's tears (left)
<small>PHOTOGRAPH BY BILLY STICKLAND</small>

Brian Clough (above)
<small>PHOTOGRAPH BY DAVID CANNON</small>

*T*he dust settles, the wind blows and the trash flies; the scene at the
New York Giants' stadium after a big match.
An apparently uneven contest as a lone Raider is set upon by
a posse of Cowboys.

New York Giants' stadium (above)
PHOTOGRAPH BY CHRIS COLE

LA Raiders v Dallas Cowboys (right)
PHOTOGRAPH BY MIKE POWELL

*T*ackle! James Hastie of the New York Jets demonstrates
the horizontal bear hug; the Buffalo Bills'
Andre Reed is his victim.

James Hastie tackles Andre Reed
PHOTOGRAPH BY RICK STEWART

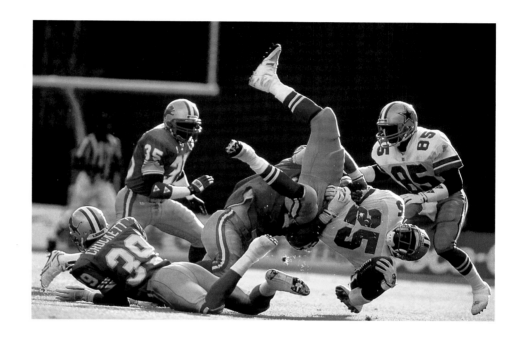

Cowboys and horses upended. Derrick Lassic of the Dallas Cowboys is sent reeling by a crunching tackle from the Detroit Lions' defence; Brown Trix falls at the infamous Becher's Brook in the 1989 Aintree Grand National.

Brown Trix (left)
PHOTOGRAPH BY BOB MARTIN

Dallas Cowboys v Detroit Lions (above)
PHOTOGRAPH BY MICHAEL COOPER

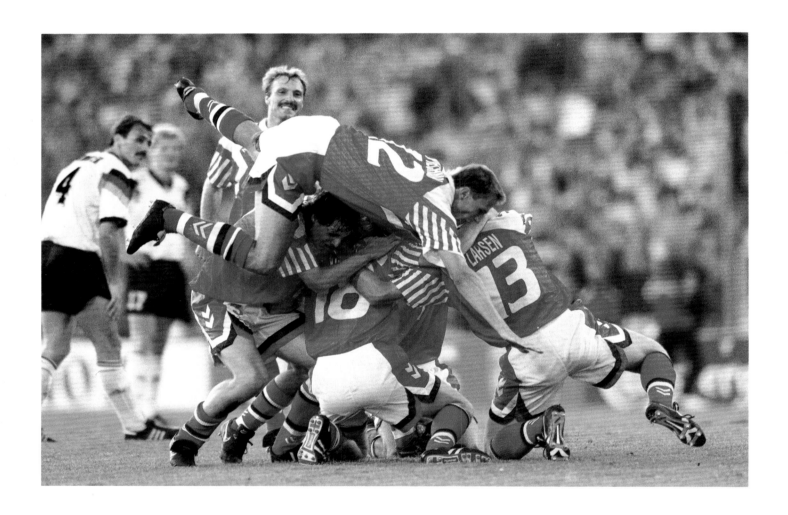

*S*omewhere at the bottom of this footballing melee is Kim Vilfort, scorer of Denmark's second goal in their

shock 2-0 victory over World Champions Germany in the 1992 European Championship Final.

Also in 1992, American Kevin Young won the Olympic 400 metre hurdles Final in Barcelona and

smashed Ed Moses' world record.

Denmark v Germany (above)
PHOTOGRAPH BY SHAUN BOTTERILL

Kevin Young (right)
PHOTOGRAPH BY BOB MARTIN

In Barcelona an unexpected bronze for Nigeria in the Women's 4 x 100 metres relay and the Spanish strike gold again as Fermin Cacho provides the 'icing on the cake' for the host nation in the 1500 metres.

Nigerian relay team (left)
PHOTOGRAPH BY BOB MARTIN

Fermin Cacho (below)
PHOTOGRAPH BY MIKE HEWITT

Triumph and tragedy in the hurdles: an emotional Kriss Akabusi has just won the 400 metre hurdles final in the European Championships at Split, establishing a new British record in the process; American Gail Devers' dreams of an Olympic Gold double in the 100 metres and the 100 metres hurdles are shattered as she hits the last barrier in the lead, and crashes across the line to finish fourth.

Gail Devers falls (left)
PHOTOGRAPHS BY JAMES MEEHAN

Kriss Akabusi (right)
PHOTOGRAPH BY SIMON BRUTY

"BEWARE WHEN THE GREAT GOD
LETS LOOSE A THINKER ON THIS PLANET"

RALPH WALDO EMERSON, 1803 – 1882

ALAIN PROST

ONE COULD SAY that all sport is like the theatre. The audience pays to watch us, the players, each performing on our own particular stage. We are celebrities, with all the advantages and disadvantages that such attention brings.

Our stage is the racetrack, but the difference from the theatre is that our text is never the same from one performance to the next. The only certainty, no matter how carefully you learn the lines, is that the outcome is unpredictable.

It is the real drama of sport and its enduring appeal that the tallest, quickest and strongest do not always end up the winners. In Formula One, so many factors play a part. It ensures that it will always be one of the most exciting of sports and spectacles.

Like a good theatre production, though, it is all too easy for the cast as well as the audience to forget how much work behind the scenes goes into a performance. Many people consider the F1 driver to be a solitary performer, but nothing could be further from the truth. You are never alone.

The team is everything. It is a motivating factor and the team ambience is vital. If the collective will is strong and positive, this will reflect in the driver's confidence. Belief in your own ability is essential, but so is belief in those around you. All aspects of F1, the technical, financial and human, are equally complex, all equally important to that final victory.

Talent and luck play a part, but the secret of success is hard work and careful preparation. You need a perfect car to win and a car is never perfect by chance, so when victory is achieved, you know that it is the team that has won.

To win races is obviously the main objective for every F1 driver, but there is more to the sport than that. Some of my best drives have been in races I haven't won and I know many drivers who feel the same. Each race is an opportunity to learn, to gather information and use that knowledge to improve.

And when you win? In just the same way, that is the time to think about the future and how to use the lessons you have learnt to make the next performance even better.

There is a tendency these days to judge a driver only by his most recent success or failure, but, like our fellow professionals on the stage, we must learn not to let our performance be affected by bad reviews.

Because, when you are part of a superb cast and know that you are turning in your best performance, you can be confident that the play will enjoy a long and successful run.

ALAIN PROST

SPA FRANCORCHAMPS · AUGUST 1993

Alain Prost, 1991
PHOTOGRAPH BY PASCAL RONDEAU

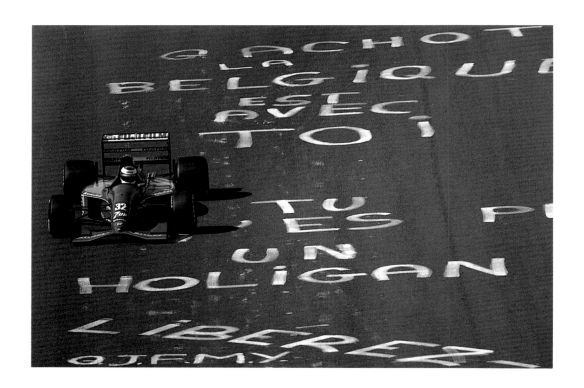

Nigel Mansell gazes through his visor at the 1991 Canadian Grand Prix. Michael Schumacher is pictured making his Formula One debut at the 1991 Belgian Grand Prix amidst a sea of graffiti protesting at the imprisonment of home driver Bertrand Gachot, whom the young German replaced.

Michael Schumacher (above)
PHOTOGRAPH BY PASCAL RONDEAU

Nigel Mansell (right)
PHOTOGRAPH BY PASCAL RONDEAU

Following his spectacular victory in the 1992 Formula One World Championship, Nigel Mansell made a successful switch to Indy Car Racing in 1993. However, Pascal Rondeau captured the moment when Mansell's first attempt at the Oval circuit ended in flames at 180 mph.

Nigel Mansell's Indy Crash

PHOTOGRAPH BY PASCAL RONDEAU

*F*ormula One driver, Mauricio Gugelmin didn't make it to the first bend at the 1989 French Grand Prix, while an oily track at Donington Park was responsible for French rider Christian Sarron's loss of control at the 1992 British Motor Cycle Grand Prix.

French Grand Prix Crash (left)
Photograph by Pascal Rondeau

Donington Park Crash (below)
Photograph by Pascal Rondeau

A lone runner is silhouetted against the rugged landscape of Vasquez Rocks in Southern California, while an English country lane and a field of rape seed provide a striking backdrop for the solo cyclist.

Running in California (left)
PHOTOGRAPH BY MIKE POWELL

The lone cyclist (below)
PHOTOGRAPH BY BOB MARTIN

Contrasting aspects and images of cycling. The 'drive for the line' is epitomised by Lance Armstrong, whilst the 'cat and mouse' impression is demonstrated by Chris Walker and Mark Walsham.

Lance Armstrong (left)
PHOTOGRAPH BY MIKE POWELL

Scottish Provident Cycling (below)
PHOTOGRAPH BY HOWARD BOYLAN

Rollerbladers speed through Boulder, Colorado on Route 36.

Rollerbladers

Photograph by Tim Defrisco

The flying Finn, Toni Nieminen on the ramp in the 120 Metre Ski Jump and Switzerland's Franz Heinzer demonstrates his mastery of the Men's Downhill.

Toni Nieminen (above)
PHOTOGRAPH BY SIMON BRUTY

Franz Heinzer (left)
PHOTOGRAPH BY CHRIS COLE

*Rocket speed perhaps (but
nothing is too fast for the
camera) the USA I Four
Man Bobsled team flashes
by in a vision of red, white
and blue.*

USA I Bobsled team

Photograph by Pascal Rondeau

Touch down for Andre Reed as the Buffalo Bills effect a come back to defeat the New York Jets 30-27. Despite the weather – Denver in December – the New York Giants fair better by beating the Broncos 14-7.

Andre Reed's touchdown, 21st October 1990 (left)
PHOTOGRAPH BY RICK STEWART

Frozen New York Giant, 10th December 1989 (below)
PHOTOGRAPH BY TIM DEFRISCO

The genius that is Michael Jordan captured in
full flow; stop him? You can try.
One man well and truly stopped, however,
is Rodney Blunt in this American college
football match as this gargantuan tackle
takes effect.

Michael Jordan (below)
PHOTOGRAPH BY JONATHAN DANIEL

North Carolina v Clemson (right)
PHOTOGRAPH BY JIM GUND

Yves Mankel and Thomas
Rudolph of Germany
donned silver suits to win
a silver medal in the Luge
Doubles at Albertville in
the 1992 Winter
Olympics.

Silver Luge
PHOTOGRAPH BY MIKE POWELL

JACKIE JOYNER KERSEE

IN MY MIND, I am a perfectionist. I always have to do better, to test myself more. If I see a picture of myself, I am always critical. If it shows me competing, then I am critical of my technique. If it's an ordinary picture, then I will be critical in a fashion sense. I know you can't be perfect, but I always feel that you must ask a lot of yourself.

This desire to achieve, to put yourself on the line and meet the challenge, is also a desire to understand yourself. It's a test of character. Where does it come from, this striving? I don't know exactly. When I was young, we were brought up in a difficult environment. There was always lots of love in the family, but we didn't have a lot in the way of material possessions. Maybe because of that you learn to appreciate what you do have, but you also strive and struggle to better yourself.

It doesn't make it easy on those around you. I am often as hard on them as I am on myself. With Bobby (my husband) though, we have worked out a perfect balance. He activates me. I want to learn as much as possible from him. On the other side, if I do relax a little or want to take it easy he won't let me.

Success cannot happen without the work. When I'm training I'm out for maybe six to eight hours a day and that may mean up to four hours on the track. I do about two hours technical work, because the javelin and the shot are my weakest events. I have to work on the mechanics of them, to slow myself down and think about what I'm doing. That's hard physically and mentally. Then you have to pull it all together for a competition.

Stuttgart was not like any competition before. Anyone can do it when they are up, but can you do it when you are down? There were real moments in Suttgart when it could all have fallen away. Then you must dig deepest, then your character is tested to the highest. To come through that is very satisfying.

Track has given me a lot in my life, but it can't be the only thing. Your horizons cannot be limited to your sport. I talk with kids a lot and tell them it is important to find a purpose in life. You must search for it and live it. At the same time, you must never lose perspective.

If you work hard and are lucky, then you may enjoy success and fulfilment. But if you come from nothing and suddenly you have substance, it is easy to get side-tracked. Even if you excel and are propelled into greatness you must not lose perspective. I try never to lose sight of where I came from.

JACKIE JOYNER KERSEE
STUTTGART · AUGUST 1993

Jackie Joyner Kersee, **World Athletics Championships, Stuttgart, 1993**
PHOTOGRAPH BY TONY DUFFY

*P*ortrait of the legendary and mischievous Bo Jackson.
On a mountain, beneath a rainbow – an appropriate pose for
the reigning Ms Olympia, Lenda Murray.

Bo Jackson's Eye (above)
PHOTOGRAPH BY JONATHAN DANIEL

Lenda Murray (right)
PHOTOGRAPH BY TONY DUFFY

*U*nity, harmony and grace: Olympian ideals symbolically demonstrated by the Ice Dancing champions, Klimova and Ponomarenko at the Albertville Winter Games.

Klimova and Ponomarenko

PHOTOGRAPH BY BOB MARTIN

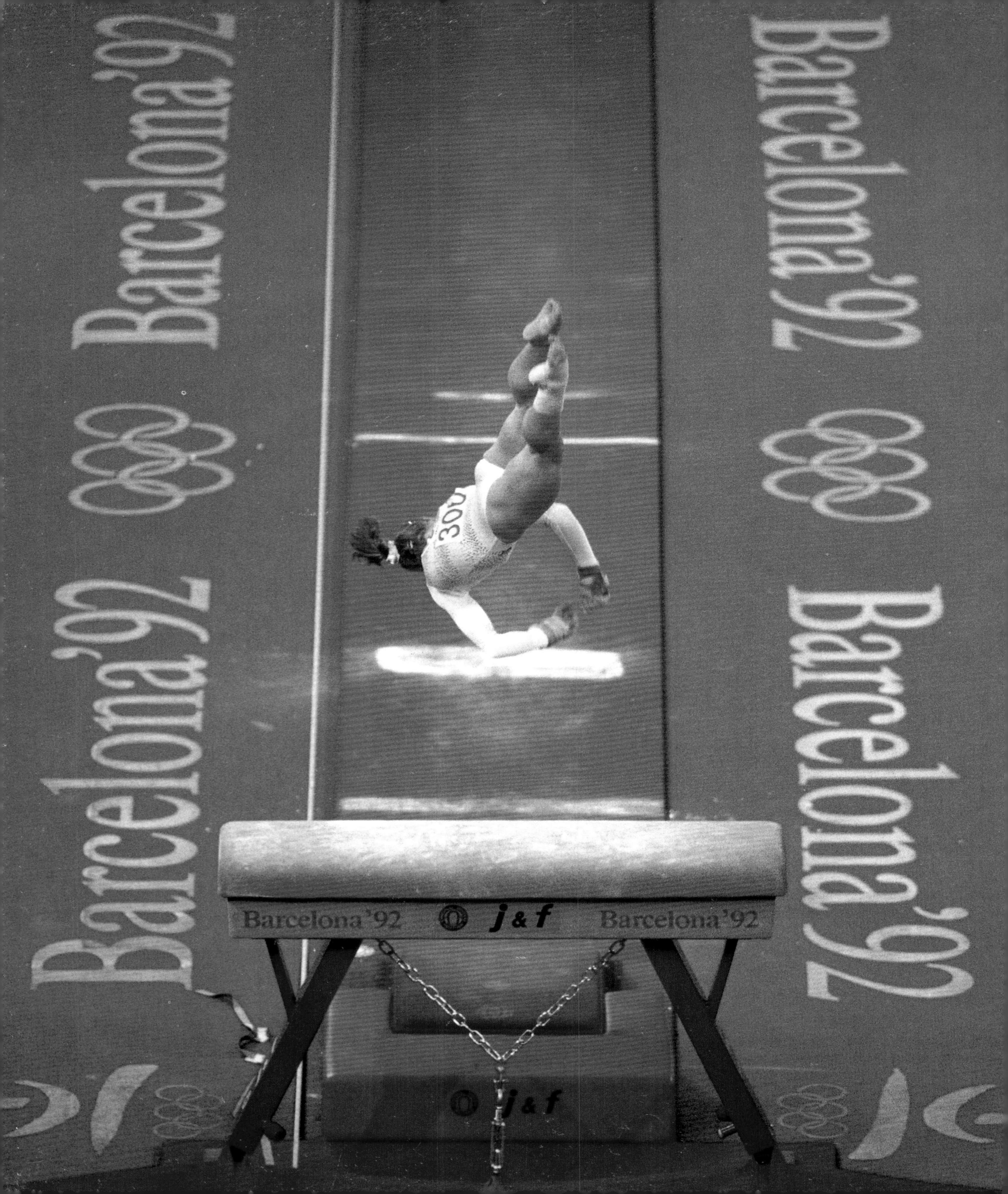
Barcelona'92
j&f
Barcelona'92
j&f

The soaring agility of the Olympic gymnast and the single-minded tenacity of the Paralympic sprinter are exemplified by Gray Mortimore's images from the 1992 Barcelona Games.

Paralympic sprinter, Peter Cordice (above)
<small>PHOTOGRAPH BY GRAY MORTIMORE</small>

Olympic gymnast, Kim Zmeskal (left)
<small>PHOTOGRAPH BY GRAY MORTIMORE</small>

Flo-Jo's Gold. Sheer ecstasy for Florence Griffith Joyner as she celebrates her victory in the Women's 100 metres Olympic Final at Seoul in 1988. Arsenal goalkeeper David Seaman is equally elated as his team reaches the FA Cup Final following a 1-0 win over arch rivals Tottenham Hotspur.

Flo-Jo (left)
PHOTOGRAPH BY STEVE POWELL

David Seaman (right)
PHOTOGRAPH BY SHAUN BOTTERILL

Jubilant German footballers celebrate their victory over Argentina in the 1990 World Cup Final in Italy, whilst Cameroon celebrates another fantastic goal on the way to the quarter finals of the same tournament.

Germany Win World Cup (left)
PHOTOGRAPH BY SIMON BRUTY

Cameroon (below)
PHOTOGRAPH BY BILLY STICKLAND

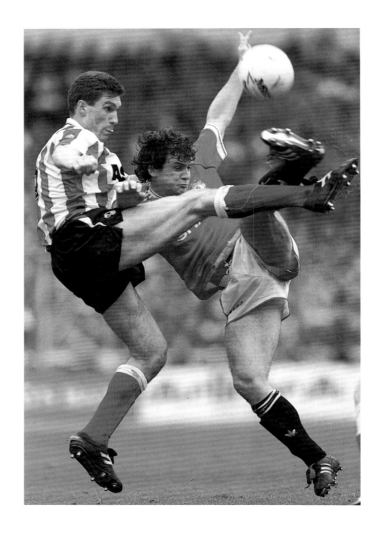

In frantic pursuit of the elusive ball: studies of the 'thrills and spills' and athleticism of English football.

Nigel Pearson and Mark Hughes (above)
PHOTOGRAPH BY SHAUN BOTTERILL

Eric Thorstvedt (right)
PHOTOGRAPH BY HOWARD BOYLAN

Sun rays and smoke flares combine to spotlight part of an expectant football crowd just minutes before the start of a match between Juventus and Inter Milan.
The Gunners' Ian Wright and Kevin Campbell celebrate their team's first goal in the 2-1 defeat of Sheffield Wednesday in the 1993 FA Cup Final Replay.

Italian Football fans (left)
PHOTOGRAPH BY SIMON BRUTY

Arsenal at Wembley (below)
PHOTOGRAPH BY SHAUN BOTTERILL

A star-spangled Magic Johnson as the much-vaunted 'Dream Team' wins the Gold Medal at the Barcelona games of 1992; Magic demonstrates his wizardry playing for the LA Lakers in 1989.

Magic Johnson and his Gold Medal (above)
PHOTOGRAPH BY MIKE POWELL

Magic Johnson of the LA Lakers (right)
PHOTOGRAPH BY STEPHEN DUNN

A cut above the rest: celebrations follow the UCLA basketball team's victory in the PAC-10 Championships. Classic Major League Baseball action during a match between the Oakland 'A's and the New York Yankees.

Basketball net cut down (below)
PHOTOGRAPH BY STEPHEN DUNN

New York Yankees v The Oakland 'A's (right)
PHOTOGRAPH BY OTTO GRUELE JR

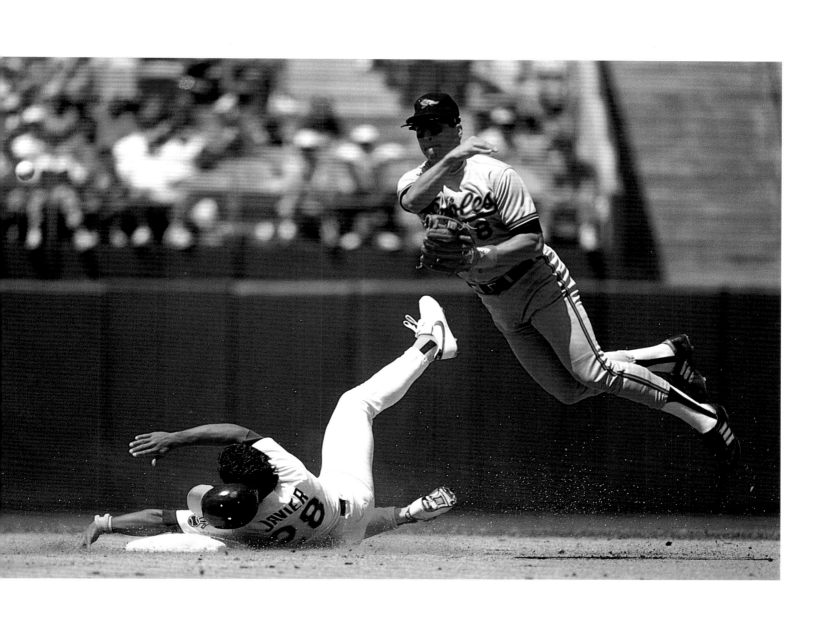

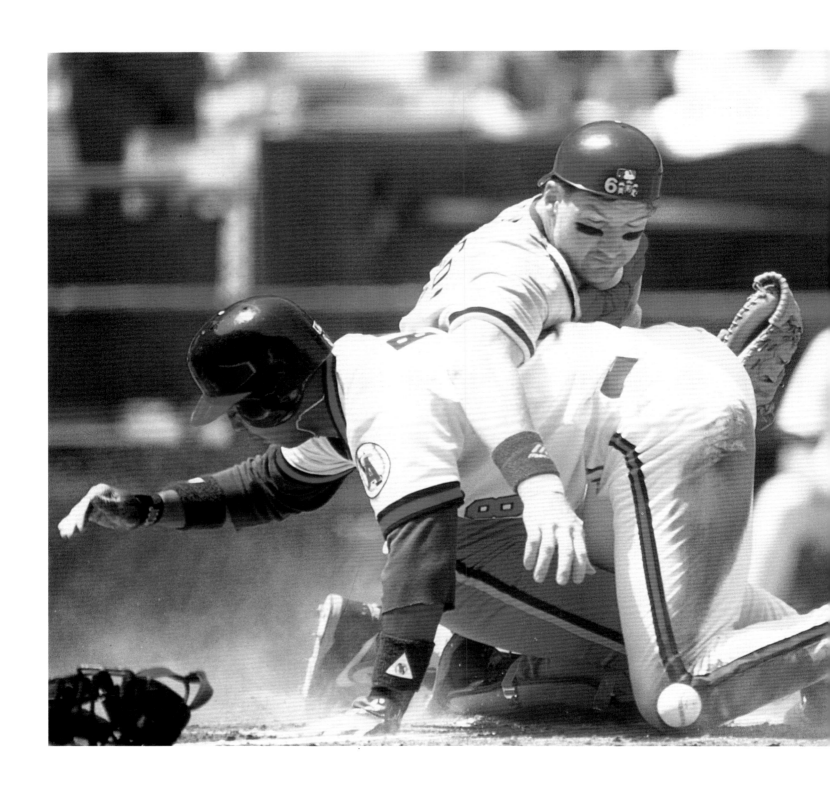

Great sporting scrambles: during a Major League Baseball game in Anaheim, California and during a 1992 Cricket World Cup semi-final in Wellington, New Zealand.

The Brewers v The Angels (left)
PHOTOGRAPH BY KEN LEVINE

New Zealand v Pakistan (below)
PHOTOGRAPH BY JOE MANN

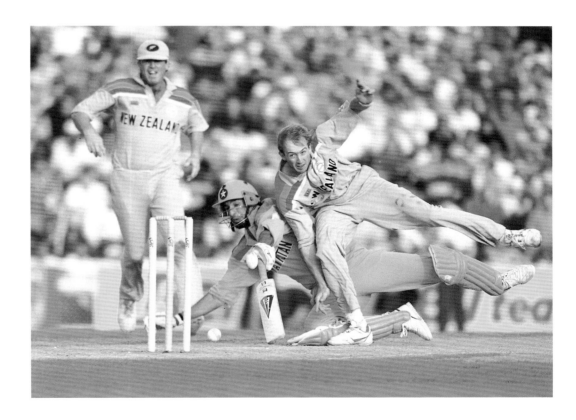

*J*ust a split second before the finger is raised. A ring of Australian fielders celebrate the fall of another English wicket during the 1989 Ashes Series.

Australian fielders

PHOTOGRAPH BY ADRIAN MURRELL

DAVID GOWER

THE OBVIOUS QUESTION would have to be whether or not the practice of 22 grown men throwing a sphere of cork and red leather at each other over a period of anything from one to five days in the name of sport without the guarantee of a decisive result constitutes the intelligent use of leisure?

Cricket is a game that has always been cited as an example of how civilised human beings can meet in earnest competition and yet uphold all the decent things in life: morals, sportsmanship, comradeship, fair play, performance of true skill and any number of other laudable ideals. Where other sports are supposed to have become 'tainted' by professionalism and commmerce, cricket is deemed an exception and supposed to set an example for all.

Actually, you only have to ponder on the selfishness of the legendary Dr W G Grace – who seemed to be able to declare himself in as and when necessary on the field and who, despite being an amateur and independently wealthy, made so much money out of the game that he would be millions ahead of today's superstars if you were prepared to make the required computations – to question how pure the game has really been.

Today, competition is as fierce as ever in the international game with no quarter being asked or given. Yet, in amongst that hard endeavour, believe it or not, the spirit of the game survives, with many of the ideals very much intact.

Individual skills and the performances of the Test playing nations will always fluctuate, but professional cricketers all round the world, have throughout history and will always, share a common love of the game that has brought them together as teammates or in opposition; a love that also binds them to a huge number of amateurs who, week in week out, play the same game entirely for fun.

Indeed the amateur spirit still breathes heavily even in the ranks of the professionals, for not everyone has converted to the creed of 'Work hard, work hard', as a philosophy, and those who still wish to play hard and enjoy it are achieving the same success that they always have done.

At a time when the clinical and exclusive pursuit of excellence is much touted in all activities, sporting or otherwise, it does us no harm to reflect that games were originally designed for the purposes of entertainment and enjoyment, aims that one should never forget, and which strike me as being both intelligent and civilised.

DAVID GOWER

HAMPSHIRE · SEPTEMBER 1993

David Gower, India v England One Day International, Bangalore, 1985
PHOTOGRAPH BY ADRIAN MURRELL

*A*ussie aggression and English anguish. Australian batsman
   Steve Waugh cuts loose at Trent Bridge during a One Day
   International match against England in 1989.
   Some six months later England captain Graham Gooch
   breaks his left hand during the team's ill-fated tour of the
   West Indies. England lost the series 2 – 1.

Steve Waugh (left)
PHOTOGRAPH BY BEN RADFORD

Graham Gooch's broken hand (below)
PHOTOGRAPH BY ADRIAN MURRELL

*S*ussex Captain Alan Wells
has just heard the sound
that every batsman dreads
as a vital wicket falls
during the 1993 Nat West
Cricket Final at Lords.

Alan Wells

Photograph by Adrian Murrell

*O*ut! *Chris Lewis is overjoyed at capturing the prize wicket of Mohammad Azharuddin during a One Day International at Jaipur; Merv Hughes looks on as Graham Gooch flicks the ball away from his stumps and in the process becomes the first English batsman to be adjudged out, 'handled the ball'.*

Chris Lewis (far left)
Photograph by Ben Radford

Gooch handles the ball (left)
Photograph by Adrian Murrell

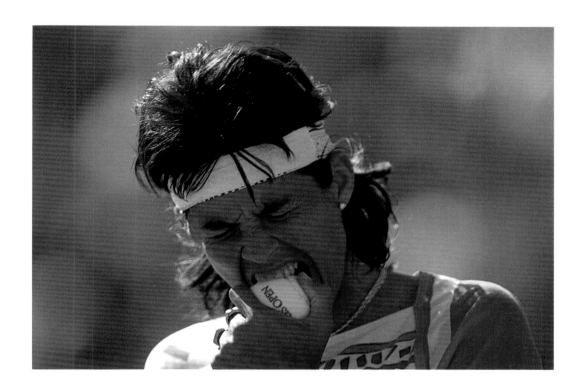

*L*eading American player Gigi Fernandez experiences some of the
agonies and frustrations of Grand Slam tennis.

Gigi Fernandez lunges in vain (left)
PHOTOGRAPH BY CHRIS COLE

Gigi Fernandez bites tennis ball (above)
PHOTOGRAPH BY DAN SMITH

Striking shades illuminate the tennis court during an evening match at Roland Garros in the 1993 French Open.

**Kenneth Carlsen
at the French Open**

Photograph by Simon Bruty

*T*wo generations of American tennis pictured at their peak. John McEnroe caught in full flight winning his third Wimbledon title in 1984 and Jim Courier's power play proving too much for fellow American Andre Agassi in the 1991 French Open.

John McEnroe (above)
PHOTOGRAPH BY STEVE POWELL

Jim Courier (right)
PHOTOGRAPH BY PASCAL RONDEAU

*An unusual view of the world's most famous tennis court;
way below, Michael Stich has just defeated Boris Becker in
Wimbledon's first all-German final of 1991.
Climbing still higher, a hot air balloon hovers over Bristol,
dwarfing the compact rows of terraced housing.*

Aerial view of Wimbledon (left)
PHOTOGRAPH BY RUSSELL CHEYNE

Ballooning (below)
PHOTOGRAPH BY BOB MARTIN

The seagull's view of a shimmering Steinlager 2, winner of the
1990 Whitbread Round the World Yacht Race.
The partial eclipse of a rugby player was witnessed
by Ben Radford during the 1991 Dubai Sevens.

Whitbread Yachting (left)
PHOTOGRAPH BY BOB MARTIN

Dubai Sevens (above)
PHOTOGRAPH BY BEN RADFORD

*T*he gliding silhouette of a speedskater and the cooling down
of a great sprinter.

Speedskater silhouette (left)
PHOTOGRAPH BY SHAUN BOTTERILL

Linford Christie cools down (above)
PHOTOGRAPH BY BOB MARTIN

*M*arathon runners in Berlin provide a symbolic moment as
thousands pass through the Brandenburg Gate. New beginnings
in Germany but a painful ending for this exhausted runner who
is treated after collapsing in the London Marathon.

Berlin Marathon (left)
PHOTOGRAPH BY BOB MARTIN

London Marathon runner (below)
PHOTOGRAPH BY MIKE COOPER

*P*utting his faith in two
colleagues and his trouser
belt, Markus Boesch clung
to a ledge of the 17th floor
of an adjacent hotel to
seize this unusual view of
Women's Beach Volleyball
in Reno, Nevada.

Women's Beach Volleyball
PHOTOGRAPH BY MARKUS BOESCH

"...WITH ALL THY WINGED SPEED"

Caroline Elizabeth Sarah Norton 1808 – 1877

RORY UNDERWOOD

IT'S NOT SOMETHING that you can rehearse. What you will do when you receive the ball in a game. There are too many options, too many possible combinations so you cannot say when *this* happens, I will do *that*. You have to rely on your own instinct, to do what you feel is right at that moment in time. If you are out wide and in a try scoring position, it may be just a matter of concentrating on staying in play, of focusing on the corner.

Natural speed obviously helps and I am lucky that I have always been, since I started playing at school in Yorkshire, reasonably quick. But that is only part of the game, there are so many other aspects to work on. Look at someone like New Zealander John Kirwan, who relies on his strength, or Australian David Campese, who is by no means the fastest of wingers, yet he has all the running skills and can beat opponents just with guile.

Having confidence in your game is vital. A few years ago, I was turning out for England and doing my best, but without any real drive or purpose.

Changes came when Geoff Cooke was appointed. He established a good management structure, squad coaching and teamwork. We started covering all aspects of the game, dissecting matches, watching videos and debating play as well as the actual training.

That preparation gives you the foundation for your confidence on the field. It can't tell you exactly what to do when – with all the coaching in the world, it's still the players who make the decisions in the end – yet it does instil a positive attitude and make you conscious of your role within the team structure. It makes you responsible and responsive. The result was two of the best years, if not the best, that England has ever had.

The years since I was first capped, against Ireland back in 1984, have gone by like the flicker of an eyelid and the records have just come, they have never been a source of motivation. I'm aware of them, but they don't dominate my thinking. I don't go around thinking, "Hooray, today I'm going to get a record", I just get on with it.

Of course I am delighted to break them, but I am only prospering from the work of others. What are the records now? It's funny, but when people ask me, often I can't remember. I know that each time I play for England, I break the record for the number of appearances and each time I score I break the try-scoring record.

RORY UNDERWOOD
LEICESTER · AUGUST 1993

Rory Underwood celebrates England's 1991 Grand Slam
PHOTOGRAPH BY RUSSELL CHEYNE

*A*n unusual golfing hazard:
Peter Senior seems unperturbed
by low-flying aircraft during
the Australian Open.

Peter Senior

PHOTOGRAPH BY JOE MANN

A profusion of azaleas creates a stunning backdrop as Seve Ballesteros contemplates a tricky putt on the fabled 13th green at Augusta. Also at the Masters, Wayne Levi extricates himself from a bunker and at the same time appears to effect the ultimate golfing trick shot.

Ballesteros and the azaleas (left)
PHOTOGRAPH BY DAVID CANNON

Wayne Levi (above)
PHOTOGRAPH BY DAVID CANNON

*T*he distinctive attire of
Payne Stewart helps to
fashion a classic golfing
image, Pebble Beach
provides the perfect
backdrop.

**Payne Stewart
at Pebble Beach**
Photograph by Stephen Dunn

*M*ixed fortunes at Augusta:
Watery duels with the
infamous Rae's Creek have
prevented Seve Ballesteros
from adding to his two
US Masters titles;
Ian Woosnam claimed his
first Major title with this
winning putt on the final
green in 1991.

Ballesteros in Rae's Creek
(left)
PHOTOGRAPH BY DAVID CANNON

Woosnam wins The Masters
(right)
PHOTOGRAPH BY STEPHEN MUNDAY

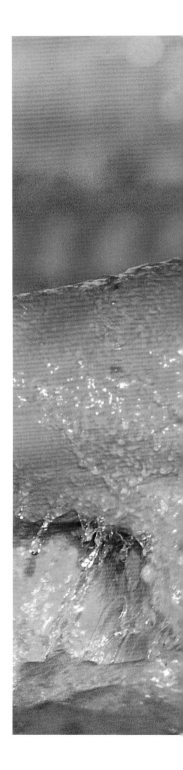

*A*n instant to breathe and a moment to celebrate for Olympic
swimming champions Melvin Stewart (butterfly) and
Daichi Suzuki (backstroke).

Daichi Suzuki (above)
PHOTOGRAPH BY SIMON BRUTY

Melvin Stewart (right)
PHOTOGRAPH BY TONY DUFFY

Concentration and calm are exhibited by this synchronised swimmer as she prepares herself during a training session at the 1992 Barcelona Olympics.

**Synchronised
Swimming Nose**

Photograph by Pascal Rondeau

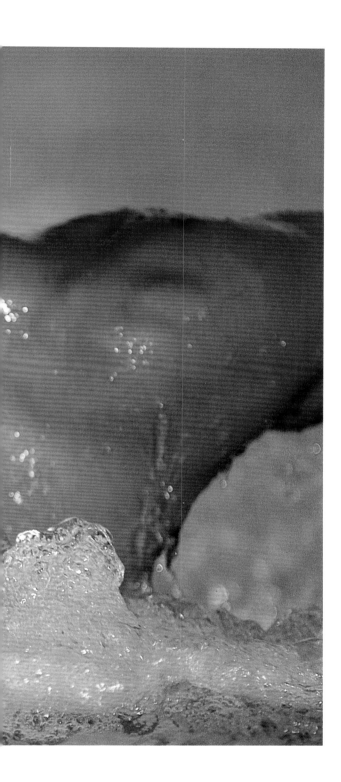

Anthony Nesty of Surinam and Alexander Popov of Russia provide studies of near-perfect symmetry in the swimming pool.

Anthony Nesty (left)
PHOTOGRAPH BY SIMON BRUTY

Alexander Popov (below)
PHOTOGRAPH BY SIMON BRUTY

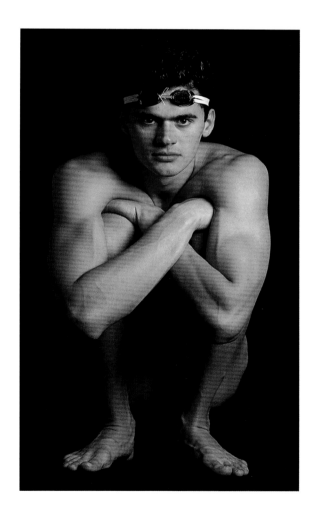

*P*arallel red lines frame and define the very contrasting sports of swimming and curling.

Lone Curler (below)
<small>PHOTOGRAPH BY MIKE HEWITT</small>

Tom Jager (right)
<small>PHOTOGRAPH BY SIMON BRUTY</small>

South Sea bubbles. The Ironman event is responsible for this extraordinary scene in the waters of Hawaii.

Ironman Triathlon in Hawaii

Photograph by Gary Newkirk

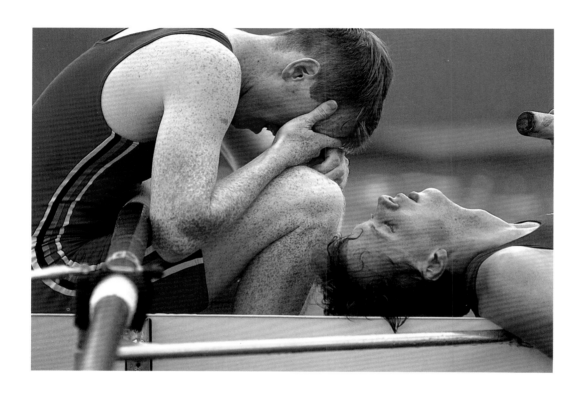

The English Summer Season: portraits of eccentricity and exhaustion at the 1993 Henley Royal Regatta.

Exhausted rowers at Henley (above)
PHOTOGRAPH BY RICHARD SAKER

Dining with the deceased (right)
PHOTOGRAPH BY RICHARD SAKER

*K*entucky rain! A heavy storm
made for exceptionally
heavy going during the
1991 Breeders Cup
Meeting. Chris Cole
captured the soggy scene
just moments before a
tractor appeared and
cleared the track.

Waterlogged Track
PHOTOGRAPH BY CHRIS COLE

"AND SAY TO ALL THE WORLD
'THIS WAS A MAN!'"

SHAKESPEARE, JULIUS CAESAR

DALEY THOMPSON

SO MUCH IN SPORT and life depends on something you have no control over, call it luck or destiny or whatever. When I started in 1975, I was in a sport that no one took any notice of and within that sport I was doing an event that no one had ever heard of. I was seriously in the back of nowhere.

Then along came Coe, Cram and Ovett and they gave my sport the highest profile for any sport in the country. They took athletics off the back pages and put it on the front pages. But for those three, I wouldn't have become as well known as I have. So I was lucky to be around at the same time.

Sure, I was dedicated too. I figured there was only one way to do it and that was to put 105 per cent effort into it, to the exclusion of everything. There's any number of people in the world that have talent, but only a very few who make something of it.

I'm a realist, I know my strengths and weaknesses, and I've always known about the people I've competed against too, but I also felt sure about my ability to compete. If I was nervous before a competition, it was not because I was worried, rather it was a sense of anticipation. There was never a time when I thought anyone could beat me.

Things change though and when we started the family, decathlon moved from being my whole life to something smaller. Now my family is the most important thing I have.

When your career is happening, you don't necessarily take it all in. Your viewpoint is a very particular one, you are centred on what you are doing. When I look back at photographs of those moments, in Los Angeles or Helsinki or wherever, it's not always what's in the picture that's important. Often, the photograph reminds you of something that isn't in the frame. Reminds you of the things that were happening around you, that flickered in and out of the main picture.

I'm still very competitive, but I don't linger in the past because there's still plenty of life to live. Sport, as I see it, is about making the most of now and never being an "I could have or I might have been."

DALEY THOMPSON

LONDON · SEPTEMBER 1993

Daley Thompson, World Athletics Championships, Rome 1987
PHOTOGRAPH BY GRAY MORTIMORE

An extraordinary resolve has guided Nick Faldo's climb to the pinnacle of world golf. The Englishman is the only player to have won both The Masters at Augusta and The Open Championship at St Andrews in the same calendar year.

Nick Faldo (above)
PHOTOGRAPH BY DAVID CANNON

Red Arrows over St Andrews (right)
PHOTOGRAPH BY SIMON BRUTY

Two of Europe's leading golfers, Nick Faldo and José-Maria Olazabal express contrasting emotions after respectively holing and missing crucial putts.

Olazabal misses at the Scottish Open, Gleneagles, 1990 (right)
PHOTOGRAPH BY DAVID CANNON

Faldo's final putt at the US Open, Pebble Beach, 1992 (below)
PHOTOGRAPH BY GARY NEWKIRK

*S*hadows that stalk and shadows that walk. Similar effects but contrasting goals are evident at the Annual
Bull Fight in Nimes and the World Race Walking Championships at L'Hospitalet, France.

The Bullfight (left)
PHOTOGRAPH BY PASCAL RONDEAU

The Walkers (above)
PHOTOGRAPH BY DAN SMITH

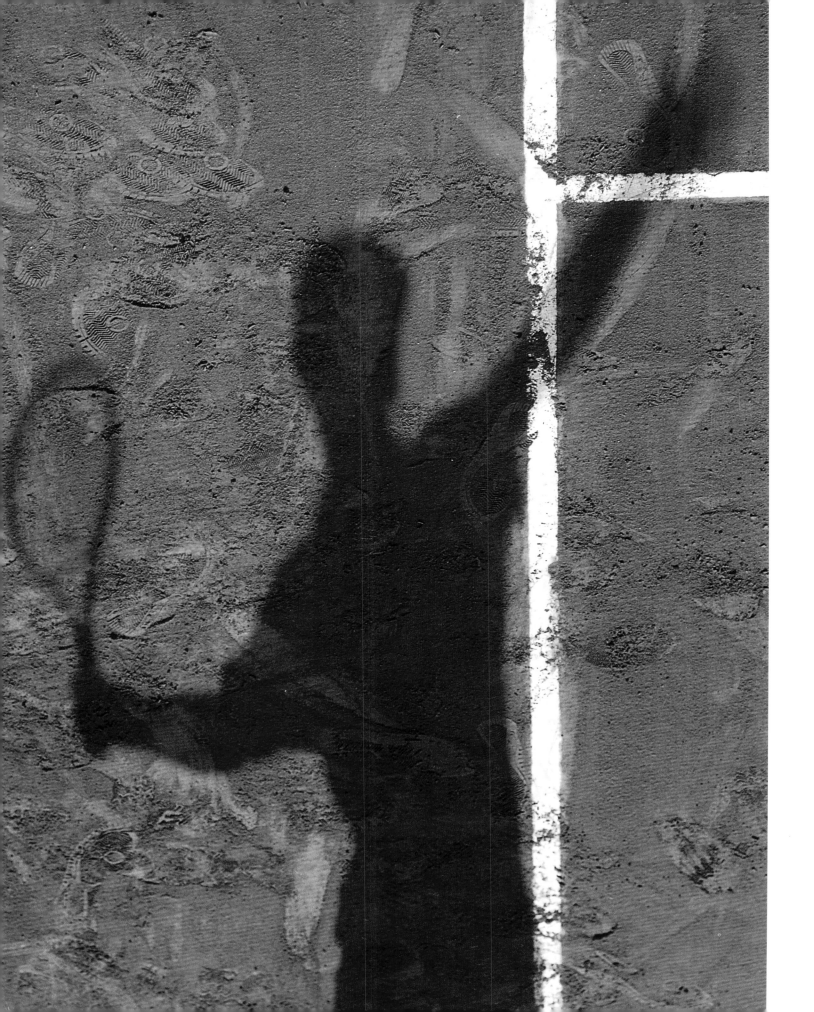

A *ghostly serve on clay and a legendary dive on grass. A classic Boris*
Becker lunge at Wimbledon provides a perfect contrast to the
Roland Garros apparition.

The tennis ghost (left)
PHOTOGRAPH BY GARY M PRIOR

Boris Becker diving (above)
PHOTOGRAPH BY CHRIS COLE

*P*oetry in motion. Two-year old 'wonder horse', Arazi, storms to a brilliant victory in the 1991 Breeders Cup Meeting at Kentucky.

Arazi
PHOTOGRAPH BY CHRIS COLE

Dedication: a poorly-lit deserted garage in East LA serves as a most unlikely – almost sinister – gym for boxer Oscar de la Hoya. Strength, balance and poise are displayed by gymnast Terry Bartlett.

Oscar de la Hoya (left)
PHOTOGRAPH BY MIKE POWELL

Terry Bartlett (right)
PHOTOGRAPH BY PASCAL RONDEAU

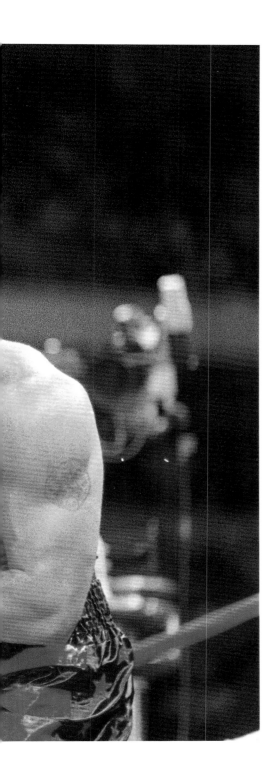

Heavyweights through the ages. A bridge too far for former Heavyweight Champion George Foreman as he suffers at the hands of Tommy Morrison. Britain's first World Heavyweight Champion this century, Lennox Lewis, raises his arms aloft following a knock-out victory over Razor Ruddock.

George Foreman (left)
PHOTOGRAPH BY MARC MORRISON

Lennox Lewis (below)
PHOTOGRAPH BY JOHN GICHIGI

Boxer Carl Daniels loses more than his dignity during a 1992 fight with Terry Norris, and rugby player Atsushi Ogagi of Japan suffers in the line out during the 1989 'friendly' match between the Universities of Cambridge and Doshiba.

Flying Gum Shield (left)
PHOTOGRAPH BY HOLLY STEIN

The Rugby Punch (below)
PHOTOGRAPH BY SIMON BRUTY

A hard fought rugby match in 1988 between London Welsh and Newport, and American footballer Hugh Williams, both provide a full head of steam.

Steaming Rugby Players (left)
PHOTOGRAPH BY CHRIS COLE

Steaming American Footballer (below)
PHOTOGRAPH BY JONATHON DANIEL

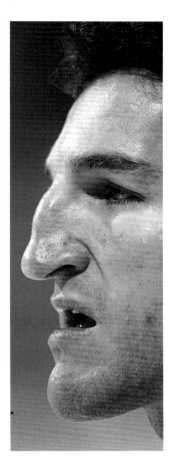

America's NHL – mayhem breaks out at the Los Angeles Forum – LA Kings' star Tim Hunter looks philosophical.

Ice hockey brawl (Left)
<small>PHOTOGRAPH BY RICK STEWART</small>

Ice hockey nose (above)
<small>PHOTOGRAPH BY MIKE POWELL</small>

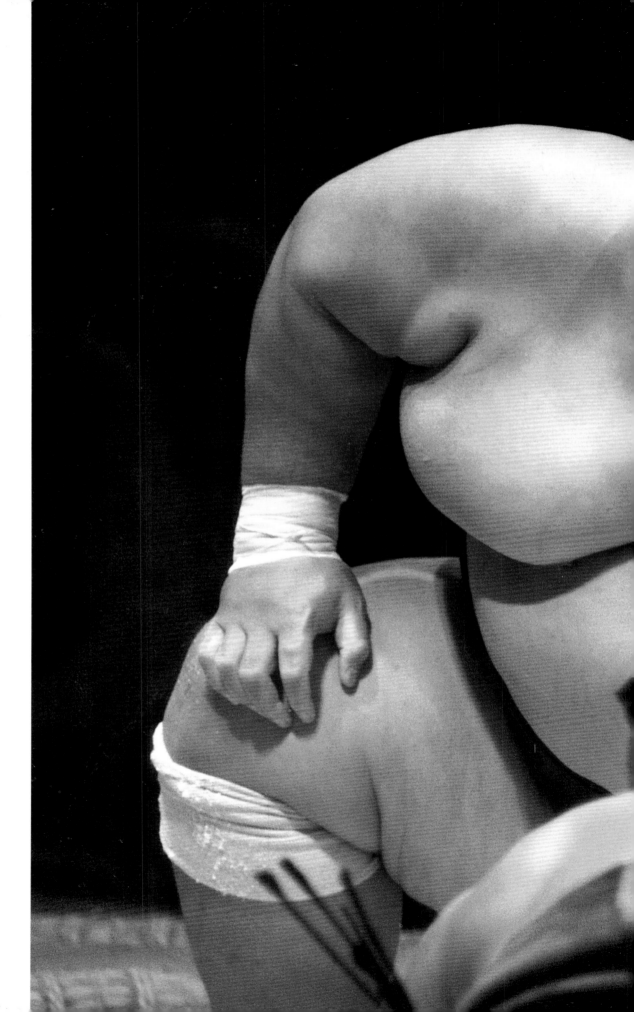

The calm before the storm.
Giant sumo wrestler,
Konishiki,
'The Dumptruck',
brought his 520lb bulk
to London's Albert Hall
in November 1991;
here he is poised to devour
his seemingly tiny
opponent, Kirishima.

Konishiki,
"The Dumptruck"
Photograph by Chris Cole

A dramatic landscape in Baja California, as trucks race over a dusty desert road.

Baja 1000 Desert Race (above)
PHOTOGRAPH BY MIKE POWELL

Carl Lewis training at the Santa Monica Track Club (right)
PHOTOGRAPH BY MIKE POWELL

ABOUT THE PHOTOGRAPHS

Ballesteros and Olazabal at the 18th
PHOTOGRAPH BY CHRIS COLE
HALF-TITLE PAGE
Ryder Cup, Kiawah Island, USA, 1991
Camera:	*Canon EOS 1*
Lens:	*Canon EOS 300mm F2.8 L*
Film:	*Fuji 100 RDP*
Exposure:	*1 / 500 at F5.6*

Olympic flame
PHOTOGRAPH BY DAVID CANNON
FRONTISPIECE
Asian Games, Seoul, 1986
Camera:	*Canon F1*
Lens:	*Canon 400 F2.8 FD*
Film:	*Fuji 100 RDP*
Exposure:	*1 / 1000 at F3.5*

Diving shadow
PHOTOGRAPH BY SIMON BRUTY
TITLE-PAGE
European Championships, Bonn, 1989
Camera:	*Canon F1*
Lens:	*Canon 400mm F2.8 FD*
Film:	*Fuji 100 RDP*
Exposure:	*1 / 1000 at F5.6*

Jana Novotna
PHOTOGRAPH BY SIMON BRUTY
PAGES 4 & 5
Australian Open, Melbourne 1991
Camera:	*Canon F1*
Lens:	*400mm F2.8 FD*
Film:	*Fuji 100 RDP*
Exposure:	*1 / 1000 at F3.5*

Bob Beamon (left)
PHOTOGRAPH BY TONY DUFFY, PAGE 6
Mexico City Olympics, 1968
Camera:	*Nikon*
Lens:	*180mm*
Film:	*Kodak TRI-X*
Exposure:	*1 / 500 at F8*

Mike Powell World Record (right)
PHOTOGRAPH BY MIKE POWELL, PAGE 9
World Championships, Tokyo, 1991
Camera:	*Canon EOS 1*
Lens:	*Canon EOS 80-200mm F2.8 L*
Film:	*Fuji 1600 neg*
Exposure:	*1 / 500 at F2.8*

Tracey Miles diving over Barcelona
PHOTOGRAPH BY BOB MARTIN
PAGES 10 & 11
Barcelona Olympics, 1992
Camera:	*Hasselblad + Strobes*
Lens:	*100mm + Polarising Filter*
Film:	*Fuji 100 RDP*
Exposure:	*1 / 500 at F8*

Houston pole vault
PHOTOGRAPH BY TIM DEFRISCO, PAGE 12
TAC Championships Houston, 1989
Camera:	*Canon F1*
Lens:	*Canon 400mm F2.8 FD*
Film:	*Fuji 100 RDP*
Exposure:	*1 / 500 at F8*

Sepak Takraw
PHOTOGRAPH BY MIKE POWELL, PAGE 13
Foot Volleyball, Malibu, California, 1991
Camera:	*Canon EOS 1 + Norman Flashes*
Lens:	*Canon EOS 20-25mm 2.8 L*
Film:	*Fuji Velvia*
Exposure:	*1 / 250 at F8*

Francis Repellin
PHOTOGRAPH BY SHAUN BOTTERILL, PAGE 14
90m Ski Jump, Albertville Olympics, 1992
Camera:	*Nikon*
Lens:	*300mm + 1.4 converter*
Film:	*Kodak EPP*
Exposure:	*1 / 30th at F5.6*

EUN Four Man Bobsled Team
PHOTOGRAPH BY SIMON BRUTY, PAGE 15
Four Man Bobsled, Albertville Olympics 1992
Camera:	*Canon EOS 1*
Lens:	*Canon EOS 400mm F2.8L*
Film:	*Kodak EPP*
Exposure:	*1 / 25 at F5.6*

Finn Jagge at Madonna
PHOTOGRAPH BY SIMON BRUTY
PAGES 16 & 17
Men's Slalom at Madonna di Campiglio, Italy, 1991
Camera:	*Canon F1*
Lens:	*Canon 300mm F2.8 FD*
Film:	*Fuji 100 RDP*
Exposure:	*1 / 1000 at F5.6*

Horse Racing on Ice
PHOTOGRAPH BY BOB MARTIN, PAGES 18 & 19
Horse Racing at St Moritz, 1989
Camera:	*Nikon*
Lens:	*500mm*
Film:	*Fuji RDP 100*
Exposure:	*1 / 1000 at F5.6*

Ice Speedway
PHOTOGRAPH BY BOB MARTIN, PAGE 20
World Ice Speedway, Frankfurt, 1991
Camera:	*Canon EOS 1*
Lens:	*Canon EOS 600mm F4 L*
Film:	*Fuji 100 RDP*
Exposure:	*1 / 2000 at F4*

Scrambling at Le Touquet
PHOTOGRAPH BY BOB MARTIN, PAGE 21
Le Touquet, France, 1992
Camera:	*Canon EOS 1*
Lens:	*Canon EOS 20-35mm F2.8 L*
Film:	*Fuji 100 RDP*
Exposure:	*1 / 1000 at F3.5*

Lone Super Bike Rider
PHOTOGRAPH BY CHRIS COLE
PAGES 22 & 23
Super Bike 1990, Donington
Camera:	*Canon F1*
Lens:	*Canon 400mm F2.8 FD*
Film:	*Fuji 100 RDP*
Exposure:	*1 / 1000 at F3.5*

Mike Powell at the 1992 Olympics
PHOTOGRAPH BY MIKE POWELL, PAGE 24
2nd place in long jump, Barcelona, 1992
Camera: Canon EOS 1
Lens: Canon EOS 200mm F1.8 L
Film: Kodak Ektapress 400
Exposure: 1 / 500 at F2.8

Andre Philips
PHOTOGRAPH BY CHRIS COLE, PAGE 26
400m hurdles, Seoul Olympics, 1988
Camera: Canon F1
Lens: Canon 400mm F2.8 FD
Film: Fuji 100 RDP
Exposure: 1 / 1000 at F4

Colin Jackson
PHOTOGRAPH BY GRAY MORTIMORE, PAGE 27
World Championships, Stuttgart, 1993
Camera: Canon EOS 1
Lens: Canon EOS 600mm F4.0 L
Film: Fuji Super G
Exposure: 1 / 500 at F4

The Searle brothers & Garry Herbert
PHOTOGRAPH BY MIKE POWELL, PAGE 28
Barcelona Olympics, 1992
Camera: Canon EOS 1
Lens: Canon EOS 500mm F4.5 L
Film: Kodak EPP
Exposure: 1 / 500 at F5.6

Dejected Cuban Wrestler
PHOTOGRAPH BY MIKE POWELL, PAGE 29
Barcelona Olympics, 1992
Camera: Canon EOS 1
Lens: Canon EOS 200mm F1.8 L
Film: Kodak Ektapress 1600
Exposure: 1 / 500 at F1.8

Greco-Roman Wrestling
PHOTOGRAPH BY SHAUN BOTTERILL
PAGES 30 & 31
90 kg event, Barcelona Olympics, 1992
Camera: Nikon
Lens: 300mm
Film: Kodak Ektapress 400
Exposure: 1 / 500 at F2

Injured hockey player
PHOTOGRAPH BY CHRIS COLE, PAGE 32
Hockey Final, Barcelona Olympics, 1992
Camera: Canon EOS 1
Lens: Canon EOS 400mm 2.8 L
Film: Kodak EPP
Exposure: 1 / 250 at F5.6

Adrian Moorhouse
PHOTOGRAPH BY TONY DUFFY, PAGE 33
100m Breaststroke, Seoul Olympics, 1988
Camera: Nikon
Lens: 400mm
Film: Kodachrome 200
Exposure: 1 / 500 at F2.8

Gazza's tears
PHOTOGRAPH BY BILLY STICKLAND, PAGE 34
World Cup, Rome, 1990
Camera: Canon EOS 1
Lens: Canon EOS 400mm F2.8 L
Film: Fuji Super G
Exposure: 1 / 500 at F2.8

Brian Clough
PHOTOGRAPH BY DAVID CANNON, PAGE 35
City Ground, Nottingham, 1993
Camera: Canon EOS 1
Lens: Canon EOS 400mm F2.8 L
Film: Fuji 1600 neg
Exposure: 1 / 250 at F2.8

New York Giants' stadium,
PHOTOGRAPH BY CHRIS COLE, PAGE 36
Super Bowl qualifier, New York, 1986
Camera: Canon T90
                  + 300TL flashgun
Lens: Canon 24mm F2.8 FD
Film: Fuji 100 RDP
Exposure: 1 / 8 at F5.6

LA Raiders v Dallas Cowboys
PHOTOGRAPH BY MIKE POWELL, PAGE 37
LA Coliseum, 1992
Camera: Canon EOS 1
Lens: Canon EOS 600mm F4 L
Film: Fuji 100 RDP
Exposure: 1 / 1000 at F4.5

James Hastie tackles Andre Reed
PHOTOGRAPH BY RICK STEWART
PAGES 38 & 39
Buffalo Bills v NY Jets, Rich Stadium,
Buffalo, 1990
Camera: Canon F1
Lens: Canon 400mm F2.8 FD
Film: Fuji RDP
Exposure: 1 / 100 at F4.5

Brown Trix
PHOTOGRAPH BY BOB MARTIN, PAGE 40
Becher's Brook, Grand National, 1989
Camera: Nikon
Lens: 35mm
Film: Fuji 100 RDP
Exposure: 1 / 1000 at F4

Dallas Cowboys v Detroit Lions
PHOTOGRAPH BY MICHAEL COOPER, PAGE 41
American Bowl, Wembley Stadium, 1993
> Camera: Canon EOS 1
> Lens: Canon EOS 300mm F2.8 L
> + Canon EOS 1.4 converter
> Film: Fuji 100 RDP
> Exposure: 1 / 500 at F4

Denmark v Germany
PHOTOGRAPH BY SHAUN BOTTERILL, PAGE 42
European Ch/ship Final, Sweden, 1992
> Camera: Nikon
> Lens: 400mm
> Film: Fuji 1600 Neg
> Exposure: 1 / 500 at F2.8

Kevin Young
PHOTOGRAPH BY BOB MARTIN, PAGE 43
400m hurdles, Barcelona Olympics, 1992
> Camera: Canon EOS 1
> Lens: Canon EOS 600mm F4 L
> Film: Kodak Ektapress 400
> Exposure: 1 / 500 at F4

Nigerian relay team
PHOTOGRAPH BY BOB MARTIN, PAGE 44
4x100m final, Barcelona Olympics, 1992
> Camera: Canon EOS 1
> Lens: Canon EOS 400mm F2.8 L
> Film: Kodak 400 Ektapress
> Exposure: 1 / 500 at F4

Fermin Cacho
PHOTOGRAPH BY MIKE HEWITT, PAGE 45
1500m final, Barcelona Olympics, 1992
> Camera: Canon EOS 1
> Lens: Canon EOS 600mm F4 L
> Film: Kodak Ektapress 400
> Exposure: 1 / 250 at F4

Gail Devers falls (sequence)
PHOTOGRAPHS BY JAMES MEEHAN, PAGE 46
100m final, Barcelona Olympics, 1992
> Camera: Canon EOS 1
> Lens: Canon EOS 600mm F4.L
> Film: Kodak Ektapress 400
> Exposure: 1 / 500 at F4

Kriss Akabusi
PHOTOGRAPH BY SIMON BRUTY, PAGE 47
European Championships, Split, 1990
> Camera: Canon EOS 1
> Lens: Canon EOS 20-35mm F2.8L
> Film: Fuji Super HG
> Exposure: 1 / 250 at F3.5

Alain Prost, 1991
PHOTOGRAPH BY PASCAL RONDEAU, PAGE 48
> Camera: Canon EOS 1
> Lens: Canon EOS 200mm F1.8 L
> + Canon EOS 1.4 converter
> Film: Fuji 100 RDP
> Exposure: 1 / 125 at F2.8

Michael Schumacher
PHOTOGRAPH BY PASCAL RONDEAU, PAGE 50
Belgian Grand Prix, Spa, 1991
> Camera: Nikon
> Lens: 500mm
> Film: Fuji 100 RDP
> Exposure: 1 / 1000 at F4

Nigel Mansell
PHOTOGRAPH BY PASCAL RONDEAU, PAGE 51
Canadian Grand Prix, Montreal, 1991
> Camera: Canon EOS 1
> Lens: 300mm
> Film: Fuji 100 RDP
> Exposure: 1 / 250 at F 2.8

Nigel Mansell's Indy Crash
PHOTOGRAPH BY PASCAL RONDEAU
PAGES 52 & 53
Phoenix Indy Car Race, Arizona,1993
> Camera: Canon EOS 1
> Lens: Canon EOS 200mm F1.8L
> Film: Fuji 100 RDP
> Exposure: 1 / 250 at F11

French Grand Prix Crash
PHOTOGRAPH BY PASCAL RONDEAU, PAGE 54
Paul Ricard Circuit, French Grand Prix,
1989
> Camera: Nikon
> Lens: 300mm
> Film: Fuji 100 RDP
> Exposure: 1 / 500 at F5.6

Donington Park Crash
PHOTOGRAPH BY PASCAL RONDEAU, PAGE 55
British Motor Cycle Grand Prix, 1992
> Camera: Canon EOS 1
> Lens: Canon EOS 200mm 1.8L
> + Canon EOS 1.4 converter
> Film: Fuji 100 RDP
> Exposure: 1 / 125 at F16

Running in California
PHOTOGRAPH BY MIKE POWELL, PAGE 56
Vasquez Rocks near LA, 1991
> Camera: Canon EOS 1
> Lens: Canon 80-200mm F2.8 L
> Film: Fuji Velvia
> Exposure: 1 / 500 at F5.6

Lone cyclist
PHOTOGRAPH BY BOB MARTIN, PAGE 57
Dave Rainer, Yorkshire, 1990
> Camera: Nikon
> Lens: 300mm
> Film: Fuji 100 RDP
> Exposure: 1 / 15 at F11

Lance Armstrong
PHOTOGRAPH BY MIKE POWELL, PAGE 58
Tour du Pont, USA, 1993
Camera: *Canon EOS 1*
Lens: *Canon EOS 200mm F1.8 L*
        + EOS 1.4 Converter
Film: *Fuji 100 RDP*
Exposure: *1 / 500 at F5.6*

Scottish Provident Cycling
PHOTOGRAPH BY HOWARD BOYLAN, PAGE 59
Camera: *Canon T90*
Lens: *Canon 300mm 2.8 FD*
Film: *Fuji 100 RDP*
Exposure: *1 / 500 at F2.8*

Rollerbladers
PHOTOGRAPH BY TIM DEFRISCO,
PAGES 60 & 61
Boulder, Colorado, 1991
Camera: *Canon EOS 1*
Lens: *Canon EOS 400mm F2.8L*
Film: *Velvia*
Exposure: *1 / 1000 at F2.8*

Franz Heinzer
PHOTOGRAPH BY CHRIS COLE, PAGE 62
Men's Downhill, Albertville Olympics,
1992
Camera: *Canon EOS 1*
Lens: *Canon EOS 400mm F2.8L*
Film: *Kodak EPP*
Exposure: *1 / 1000 at F5.6*

Toni Nieminen
PHOTOGRAPH BY SIMON BRUTY, PAGE 63
120m Ski Jump, Albertville Olympics,
1992
Camera: *Canon EOS 1*
Lens: *Canon EOS 400mm F2.8L*
Film: *Kodak EPP*
Exposure: *1 / 60 at F5.6*

USA 1 Bobsled team
PHOTOGRAPH BY PASCAL RONDEAU
PAGES 64 & 65
Four Man Bob, Albertville Olympics, 1992
Camera: *Canon EOS 1*
Lens: *Canon EOS 300mm F2.8L*
Film: *Kodak EPP*
Exposure: *1 / 60 at F18*

Andre Reed's touchdown
PHOTOGRAPH BY RICK STEWART, PAGE 66
Buffalo Bills v New York Jets, Buffalo, NY,
1990
Camera: *Canon F1*
Lens: *Canon 50mm F1.8 FD*
Film: *Fuji RDP*
Exposure: *1 / 1000 at F3.5*

Frozen New York Giant
PHOTOGRAPH BY TIM DEFRISCO, PAGE 67
Giants v Broncos, Denver, CO, 1989
Camera: *Canon F1*
Lens: *Canon 24mm F2.8 FD*
Film: *Kodachrome 200*
Exposure: *1 / 125 at F2.8*

Michael Jordan
PHOTOGRAPH BY JONATHAN DANIEL, PAGE 68
NBA Finals, Bulls v Lakers, Chicago, 1991
Camera: *Nikon*
Lens: *135mm*
Film: *Kodak Ektapress 1600*
Exposure: *1 / 500 at F2.8*

North Carolina v Clemson
PHOTOGRAPH BY JIM GUND, PAGE 69
Clemson, South Carolina, 1992
Camera: *Canon F1*
Lens: *Canon 400mm F2.8 FD*
Film: *Fuji RDP*
Exposure: *1 / 1000 at F2.8*

Silver Luge
PHOTOGRAPH BY MIKE POWELL
PAGES 70 & 71
Yves Mankel and Thomas Rudolph,
Luge doubles, Albertville Olympics, 1992
Camera: *Canon EOS 1*
Lens: *Canon EOS 500mm F4.5 L*
Film: *Kodak EPP*
Exposure: *1 / 500 at F5.6*

Jackie Joyner Kersee
PHOTOGRAPH BY TONY DUFFY, PAGE 72
World Championships, Stuttgart, 1993
Camera: *Canon EOS 1*
        + 430 EZ Flash
Lens: Canon EOS 20-35mm F2.8 L
Film: *Fuji Super G*
Exposure: *1 / 250 at F4*

Bo Jackson's Eye
PHOTOGRAPH BY JONATHAN DANIEL, PAGE 74
Chicago White Sox, Illinois, 1991
Camera: *Nikon*
Lens: *400mm*
Film: *Fuji RDP*
Exposure: *1 / 500 at F2.8*

Lenda Murray
PHOTOGRAPH BY TONY DUFFY, PAGE 75
Chatsworth, California
Camera: *Canon EOS 1*
        + Speedlight 430 E2
Lens: *Canon EOS 20-30 F2.8L*
Film: *Fuji Velvia*
Exposure: *1 / 250 at F8*

Klimova and Ponomarenko
PHOTOGRAPH BY BOB MARTIN
PAGES 76 & 77
Ice Dancing, Albertville Olympics, 1992
Camera: Canon EOS 1
Lens: Canon EOS 85mm F1.8L
Film: Kodachrome 200
Exposure: 1 / 500 at F2.8

Olympic Gymnast, Kim Zmeskal
PHOTOGRAPH BY GRAY MORTIMORE, PAGE 78
Barcelona Olympics, 1992
Camera: Canon EOS 1
Lens: Canon EOS 400 2.8L
Film: Kodak Ektapress 400
Exposure: 1 / 640 at F2.8

Paralympic Sprinter, Peter Cordice
PHOTOGRAPH BY GRAY MORTIMORE, PAGE 79
Paralympic Games, Barcelona, 1992
Camera: Canon EOS 1
Lens: Canon EOS 400 2.8L
Film: Kodak Ektapress 1600
Exposure: 1 / 640 at F3.2

Flo-Jo
PHOTOGRAPH BY STEVE POWELL, PAGE 80
100m final, Seoul Olympics, 1988
Camera: Nikon
Lens: 600mm
Film: Ektachrome 64X
Exposure: 1 / 1000 at F4.5

David Seaman
PHOTOGRAPH BY SHAUN BOTTERILL, PAGE 81
FA Cup Semi-final, Wembley, 1993
Camera: Nikon
Lens: 400mm
Film: Fuji RDP
Exposure: 1 / 500 at F5.6

Germany Win World Cup
PHOTOGRAPH BY SIMON BRUTY, PAGE 82
World Cup Final, Italy, 1990
Camera: Canon EOS 1
                    + Canon 430 EZ
Lens: EOS 20-35mm 2.8L
Film: Fuji Super HG
Exposure: 1 / 8 at F11

Cameroon
PHOTOGRAPH BY BILLY STICKLAND, PAGE 83
World Cup, Italy, 1990
Camera: Canon EOS 1
Lens: Canon EOS 400mm F2.8L
Film: Fuji Super G
Exposure: 1 / 500 at F2.8

Nigel Pearson and Mark Hughes
PHOTOGRAPH BY SHAUN BOTTERILL, PAGE 84
League Cup Final, Wembley, 1991
Camera   Nikon
Lens: 400 2.8mm
Film: Fuji Super HG
Exposure: 1 / 500 at F2.8

Eric Thorstvedt
PHOTOGRAPH BY HOWARD BOYLAN, PAGE 85
Spurs v Aston Villa, London, 1991
Camera: Canon T90
Lens: Canon 300 2.8 FD
Film: Fuji Super HG
Exposure: 1 / 1000 at F2.8

Italian Football Fans
PHOTOGRAPH BY SIMON BRUTY, PAGE 86
Juventus v Inter Milan, Turin, Italy, 1992
Camera: Canon EOS 1
Lens: Canon EOS 400mm F2.8L
Film: Fuji Velvia
Exposure: 1 / 500 at F5.6

Arsenal at Wembley
PHOTOGRAPH BY SHAUN BOTTERILL, PAGE 87
FA Cup Final Replay, London, 1993
Camera: Nikon
Lens: 400mm
Film: Fuji Super G
Exposure: 1 / 500 at F2.8

Magic Johnson and his Gold Medal
PHOTOGRAPH BY MIKE POWELL, PAGE 88
Barcelona Olympics, 1992
Camera: Canon EOS 1
Lens: Canon EOS 400mm F2.8 L
Film: Kodak Ektapress 400
Exposure: 1 / 250 at F4

Magic Johnson of the LA Lakers
PHOTOGRAPH BY STEPHEN DUNN, PAGE 89
Great Western, LA Forum, 1989
Camera:	Nikon + strobes
Lens:	85mm
Film:	Fuji 100 RDP
Exposure:	1 / 250 at F4

Basketball net cut down
PHOTOGRAPH BY STEPHEN DUNN, PAGE 90
PAC-10 Championships, LA, 1992
Camera:	Nikon
	+ stadium strobe lighting
Lens:	35m
Film:	Fuji 100 RDP
Exposure:	1 / 250 at F4.0

New York Yankees v The Oakland 'A's
PHOTOGRAPH BY OTTO GREULE JNR, PAGE 91
Major League Baseball, California, 1989
Camera:	Nikon F3
Lens:	500 F4
Film:	Fuji RDP 100
Exposure	1 / 1000 at F5.6

The Brewers v The Angels
PHOTOGRAPH BY KEN LEVINE, PAGE 92
Major League Baseball, California, 1992
Camera:	Canon EOS 1
Lens:	Canon 600mm F4 L
Film:	Fuji RDP
Exposure:	1 / 1000 at F4

New Zealand v Pakistan
PHOTOGRAPH BY JOE MANN, PAGE 93
World Cup Cricket, New Zealand, 1991
Camera:	Nikon
Lens:	600mm
Film:	Kodak Ektapress 400
Exposure:	1 / 500 at F4.0

Australian fielders
PHOTOGRAPH BY ADRIAN MURRELL
PAGES 94 & 95
The Ashes, England, June 1989
Camera:	Nikon F3
Lens:	300mm F5.6
Film:	Fuji 100 RDP
Exposure:	1 / 500 at F5.6

David Gower
PHOTOGRAPH BY ADRIAN MURRELL, PAGE 96
India v England, Bangalore, 1985
Camera:	Nikon
Lens:	600mm + 1.4 converter
Film:	Fuji 100
Exposure:	1 / 1000 at F5.6

Steve Waugh
PHOTOGRAPH BY BEN RADFORD, PAGE 98
2nd One Day International,
England v Australia, 1989
Camera:	Canon F1
Lens:	Canon 800mm F5.6 FD
	+ 1.4 FD converter
Film:	Fuji 100 RDP
Exposure:	1 / 500 at F5.6

Gooch's Broken Hand
PHOTOGRAPH BY ADRIAN MURRELL, PAGE 99
3rd Test, West Indies v England, Trinidad,
1990
Camera:	Nikon
Lens:	600mm + 1.4 converter
Film:	Kodak 400 Ektapress
Exposure:	1 / 500 at F5.6

Alan Wells
PHOTOGRAPH BY ADRIAN MURRELL
PAGES 100 & 101
Nat West Final, Lords, 1993
Camera:	Canon EOS 1
Lens:	Canon 600mm F4 L
Film:	Fuji Super G
Exposure:	1 / 800 at F5.6

Chris Lewis
PHOTOGRAPH BY BEN RADFORD, PAGE 102
1st One Day International, Jaipur, India,
1993
Camera:	Canon F1
Lens:	Canon 800mm F5.6 FD
Film:	Kodak 160 Gold
Exposure:	1 / 1000 at F5.6

Gooch handles the ball
PHOTOGRAPH BY ADRIAN MURRELL, PAGE 103
England v Australia 1st Test, Manchester,
1993
Camera:	Canon EOS 1
Lens:	Canon EOS 600mm F4.0L
	+1.4 Canon EOS converter
Film:	Fuji Super G 400
Exposure:	1 / 500 at F5.6

Gigi Fernandez lunges in vain
PHOTOGRAPH BY CHRIS COLE, PAGE 104
French Open, Roland Garros, 1992
Camera:	Canon EOS 1
Lens:	Canon 400mm F2.8L
Film:	Fuji 100 RDP
Exposure:	1 / 1000 at F4.5

Gigi Fernandez bites tennis ball
PHOTOGRAPH BY DAN SMITH, PAGE 105
US Open, Flushing Meadow, NYC, 1991
Camera:	Nikon
Lens:	500mm
Film:	Fuji 100 RDP
Exposure:	1 / 500 at F4

Kenneth Carlsen at the French Open
PHOTOGRAPH BY SIMON BRUTY
PAGES 106 & 107
French Open, Roland Garros, Paris, 1993
Camera:	Canon EOS 1
Lens:	Canon EOS 28-80mm
	F2.8L-4 L
Film:	Fuji Velvia
Exposure:	1 / 500 at F4

John McEnroe
PHOTOGRAPH BY STEVE POWELL, PAGE 108
Wimbledon, England, 1984
Camera:	Nikon F3
Lens:	200mm
Film:	Kodak Ektachrome 64X
Exposure:	1 / 1000 at F4

Jim Courier
PHOTOGRAPH BY PASCAL RONDEAU, PAGE 109
French Open Final v Andre Agassi, Roland
Garros, Paris, 1991
Camera:	Canon EOS 1
Lens:	Canon EOS 600mm F4.0L
Film:	Fuji 100 RDP
Exposure:	1 / 500 at F5.6

Aerial view of Wimbledon
PHOTOGRAPH BY RUSSELL CHEYNE, PAGE 110
Men's Final, Stich beats Becker, 1991
Camera:	Nikon
Lens:	85mm
Film:	Fuji 100 RDP
Exposure:	1 / 1000 at F3.5

Ballooning
PHOTOGRAPH BY BOB MARTIN, PAGE 111
Bristol Balloon Festival, England, 1990
Camera:	Canon EOS 1
Lens:	Canon EOS 80-200 F2.8 L
Film :	Fuji 100 RDP
Exposure:	1 / 1000 at F4

Whitbread Yachting
PHOTOGRAPH BY BOB MARTIN, PAGE 112
Whitbread Round The World Race, 1990
Camera:	Nikon
Lens:	80-200mm
Film:	Fuji 100 RDP
Exposure:	1 / 1000 at F5.6

Dubai Sevens
PHOTOGRAPH BY BEN RADFORD, PAGE 113
Dubai Sevens rugby tournament, UAE,
1991
Camera:	Canon F1
Lens:	Canon 400mm F2.8 FD
	+ Canon FD 1.4 converter
Film:	Fuji 100 RDP
Exposure:	1 / 250 at F4.0

Speedskater silhouette
PHOTOGRAPH BY SHAUN BOTTERILL, PAGE 114
Albertville Olympics, 1992
Camera:	Nikon
Lens:	300mm
Film:	Kodak EPP
Exposure:	1 / 1000 at F5.6

Linford Christie cools down
PHOTOGRAPH BY BOB MARTIN, PAGE 115
Allsport studio shoot, 1991
Camera:	Canon EOS 1
	+ Studio Lights
Lens:	Canon EOS 300mm 2.8 L
Film:	Fuji 100 RDP
Exposure	1 / 250 at F11

Berlin Marathon
PHOTOGRAPH BY BOB MARTIN, PAGE 116
Berlin, Germany, 1990
Camera:	Canon EOS 1
Lens:	Canon EOS 80-200mm
	F2.8 L
Film:	Fuji 100 RDP
Exposure:	1 / 500 at F2.8

London Marathon runner
PHOTOGRAPH BY MIKE COOPER, PAGE 117
NutraSweet London Marathon, 1993
Camera:	Canon EOS 1
Lens:	Canon EOS 24mm 2.8
Film:	Fuji Velvia
Exposure:	1 / 250 at F5.6

Women's Beach Volleyball
PHOTOGRAPH BY MARKUS BOESCH
PAGES 118 & 119
Reno, Nevada, USA, 1991
Camera:	Nikon
Lens:	200mm
Film:	Fuji 100 RDP
Exposure:	1 / 1000 at F5.6

**Rory Underwood celebrates England's
1991 Grand Slam**
PHOTOGRAPH BY RUSSELL CHEYNE, PAGE 120
England v France, Twickenham, 1991
Camera:	Nikon
Lens:	400mm
Film:	Fuji Neg 1600
Exposure:	1 / 500 at F2.8

Peter Senior
PHOTOGRAPH BY JOE MANN,
PAGES 122 & 123
Australian Open, Sydney, 1992
Camera:	Nikon
Lens:	200mm
Film:	Fuji 100 RDP
Exposure:	1 / 1000 at F 4.5

Ballesteros and the azaleas
PHOTOGRAPH BY DAVID CANNON,
PAGES 124 & 125
US Masters, Augusta, USA, 1992
  Camera: Canon EOS 1
  Lens: Canon EOS 600 mm F4.0L
  Film: Fuji Velvia
  Exposure: 1 / 160 at F4

Wayne Levi
PHOTOGRAPH BY DAVID CANNON, PAGE 125
US Masters, Augusta, USA, 1991
  Camera: Canon EOS 1
  Lens: Canon EOS 400mm F2.8L
  Film: Fuji Velvia
  Exposure: 1 / 500 at F3.5

Payne Stewart at Pebble Beach
PHOTOGRAPH BY STEPHEN DUNN
PAGES 126 & 127
AT&T Pebble Beach Open, California,
USA, 1991
  Camera: Nikon
  Lens: 400 mm
  Film: Fuji 100 RDP
  Exposure: 1 / 500 at F11

Ballesteros in Rae's Creek
PHOTOGRAPH BY DAVID CANNON, PAGE 128
US Masters, Augusta, USA, 1989
  Camera: Canon F1 High Speed
  Lens: 300mm F2.8 FD Canon
  Film: Fuji 100 RDP
  Exposure: 1 / 1000 at F2.8

Woosnam wins The Masters
PHOTOGRAPH BY STEPHEN MUNDAY, PAGE 129
US Masters, Augusta, USA, 1991
  Camera: Nikon
  Lens: 400mm
  Film: Fuji 100 RDP
  Exposure: 1 / 250 at F2.8

Daichi Suzuki
PHOTOGRAPH BY SIMON BRUTY, PAGE 130
Seoul Olympics, 1988
  Camera: Canon F1
  Lens: Canon 400mm F2.8FD
  Film: Kodachrome 200
  Exposure: 1 / 250 at F2.8

Melvin Stewart
PHOTOGRAPH BY TONY DUFFY, PAGE 131
Meet of Champions, MissionViejo, 1991
  Camera: Canon EOS 1
  Lens: Canon EOS 400mm 2.8L
  Film   Fuji 100 RDP
  Exposure: 1 / 1000 at F4.5

Synchronised Swimming Nose
PHOTOGRAPH BY PASCAL RONDEAU
PAGES 132 & 133
Barcelona Olympics, 1992
  Camera: EOS 1
  Lens: Canon EOS 600mm F4.0 L
  Film: Kodak EPP
  Exposure: 1 / 500 at F4.5

Anthony Nesty
PHOTOGRAPH BY SIMON BRUTY, PAGE 134
Training, University of Florida, USA
  Camera: Canon EOS 1
  Lens: Canon EOS 400mm F2.8L
  Film: Fuji Velvia
  Exposure: 1 / 1000 at F2.8

Alexander Popov
PHOTOGRAPH BY SIMON BRUTY, PAGE 135
European Swimming Championships,
Sheffield, England, 1993
  Camera: Canon EOS 1
                  + Norman flashes
  Lens: Canon EOS 80-200mm 2.8L
  Film: Fuji Velvia
  Exposure: 1 / 250 at F8

Lone Curler
PHOTOGRAPH BY MIKE HEWITT, PAGE 136
World Curling Championships, Geneva,
Switzerland, 1993
  Camera: Canon EOS 1
  Lens:Canon EOS 80-200mm F2.8L
  Film: Fuji Super HG
  Exposure: 1 / 250 at F2.8

Tom Jager
PHOTOGRAPH BY SIMON BRUTY, PAGE 137
Barcelona Olympics, 1992
  Camera: Canon EOS 1
  Lens: Canon EOS 400mm F2.8L
  Film: Kodak EPP
  Exposure: 1 / 1000 at F4.5

Ironman Triathlon in Hawaii
PHOTOGRAPH BY GARY NEWKIRK
PAGES 138 & 139
Hawaii, 1991
  Camera: Nikon
  Lens: 24mm
  Film: Fuji 100RDP
  Exposure   1 / 500 at F4

Exhausted rowers at Henley
PHOTOGRAPH BY RICHARD SAKER, PAGE 140
Henley Royal Regatta, England, 1993
  Camera: Nikon
  Lens: 300mm
  Fim: Fuji Velvia
  Exposure: 1 / 500 at F2.8

Dining with the deceased
PHOTOGRAPH BY RICHARD SAKER, PAGE 141
Henley Royal Regatta, England, 1993
  Camera: Nikon F3
  Lens: 135mm
  Film: Fuji Velvia
  Exposure: 1 / 250 at F4

Waterlogged Track
PHOTOGRAPH BY CHRIS COLE
PAGES 142 & 143
Breeders Cup, Kentucky, USA,1991
Camera:	*Canon EOS 1*
Lens:	*Canon EOS 400mm F2.8L*
Film:	*Fuji 100 RDP*
Exposure:	*1 / 500 at F4*

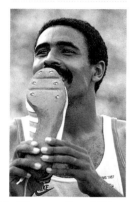

Daley Thompson, Rome 1987
PHOTOGRAPH BY GRAY MORTIMORE, PAGE 144
World Athletics Championships, 1987
Camera:	*Nikon*
Lens:	*400mm*
Film:	*Fuji 100 RDP*
Exposure:	*1 / 500 at F2.8*

Nick Faldo
PHOTOGRAPH BY DAVID CANNON, PAGE 146
World Cup of Golf by Philip Morris, Rome, 1991
Camera:	*Canon EOS 1*
Lens:	*Canon EOS 600mm F4.0L*
Film:	*Fuji Velvia*
Exposure:	*1 / 500 at F4.0*

Red Arrows over St Andrews
PHOTOGRAPH BY SIMON BRUTY, PAGE 147
The Open Championship, St Andrews, Scotland, 1990
Camera:	*Canon EOS 1*
Lens:	*Canon 20-35mm F2.8L*
Film:	*Fuji Velvia*
Exposure:	*1 / 500 at F4.5*

Nick Faldo
PHOTOGRAPH BY GARY NEWKIRK, PAGE 148
US Open, Pebble Beach, California, 1992
Camera:	*Nikon*
Lens:	*400mm*
Film:	*Fuji Velvia*
Exposure:	*1 / 500 at F3.5*

Olazabal misses at the Scottish Open
PHOTOGRAPH BY DAVID CANNON, PAGE 149
Scottish Open, Gleneagles, Scotland, 1990
Camera:	*Canon EOS 1*
Lens:	*Canon EOS 80-200mm F2.8L*
Film:	*Fuji 100 RDP*
Exposure:	*1 / 500 at F4.0*

The Bullfight
PHOTOGRAPH BY PASCAL RONDEAU, PAGE 150
Nimes, France, 1991
Camera:	*Canon EOS 1*
Lens:	*Canon EOS 600mm F4L + Canon EOS 1.4 converter*
Film:	*Fuji 100 RDP*
Exposure:	*1 / 500 at F6.3*

The Walkers
PHOTOGRAPH BY DAN SMITH, PAGE 151
World Race Walking, France, 1989
Camera:	*Nikon*
Lens:	*300mm*
Film:	*Fuji 100 RDP*
Exposure:	*1 / 500 at F4*

The tennis ghost
PHOTOGRAPH BY GARY M PRIOR, PAGE 152
French Open, Roland Garros, Paris, 1993
Camera:	*Nikon*
Lens:	*200mm*
Film:	*Fuji Velvia*
Exposure:	*1 / 500 at F2.8*

Boris Becker diving
PHOTOGRAPH BY CHRIS COLE, PAGE 153
Wimbledon, England, 1993
Camera:	*Canon EOS 1*
Lens:	*Canon EOS 80-200mm F2.8L*
Film:	*Fuji 100 RDP*
Exposure:	*1 / 500 at F3.5*

Arazi
PHOTOGRAPH BY CHRIS COLE
PAGES 154 & 155
Breeders Cup, Kentucky, USA, 1991
Camera:	*Canon EOS 1*
Lens:	*Canon EOS 20-35mm F2.8L*
Film:	*Fuji 100 RDP*
Exposure:	*1 / 2000 at F3.5*

Oscar de la Hoya
PHOTOGRAPH BY MIKE POWELL, PAGE 156
Training, California, USA, 1991
Camera:	*Canon EOS 1*
Lens:	*Canon EOS 20-35mm F2.8 L*
Film:	*Fuji 100 RDP*
Exposure:	*1 / 250 at F4.0*

Terry Bartlett
PHOTOGRAPH BY PASCAL RONDEAU, PAGE 157
Seoul Olympics, 1988

Camera:	*Nikon*
Lens:	*300mm*
Film:	*Kodak Kodachrome 200*
Exposure:	*1 / 500 at F2*

George Foreman
PHOTOGRAPH BY MARC MORRISON, PAGE 158
Las Vegas, 1993

Camera:	*Canon EOS 1*
Lens:	*Canon EOS 85mm 1.8L*
Film:	*Fuji 1600 neg*
Exposure:	*1 / 500 at F3.5*

Lennox Lewis
PHOTOGRAPH BY JOHN GICHIGI, PAGE 159
Lewis v Ruddock, England, 1992

Camera:	*Nikon*
Lens:	*400mm*
Film:	*Fuji 1600 neg*
Exposure:	*1 / 500 at F2.8*

Flying Gum Shield
PHOTOGRAPH BY HOLLY STEIN, PAGE 160
San Diego, California, 1992

Camera	*Canon F1*
Lens	*Canon 85mm 1.8L*
Film	*Fuji 1600 neg*
Exposure	*1 / 500 at F2.8*

The Rugby Punch
PHOTOGRAPH BY SIMON BRUTY, PAGE 161
Cambridge University v Doshiba
University (Japan), England, 1989

Camera:	*Canon F1*
Lens:	*Canon 400mm F2.8 FD*
Film:	*Fuji 100 RDP*
Exposure:	*1 / 500 at F2.8*

Steaming Rugby Players
PHOTOGRAPH BY CHRIS COLE, PAGE 162
London Welsh v Newport, Richmond,
1988

Camera:	*Canon F1*
Lens:	*Canon 400mm F2.8 FD*
	+ Canon 1.4 FD converter
Film:	*Fuji 100 RDP*
Exposure:	*1 / 250 at F4*

Steaming American Footballer
PHOTOGRAPH BY JONATHAN DANIEL, PAGE 163
Hugh Williams, Illinois, 1992

Camera:	*Nikon*
Lens:	*400mm*
Film:	*Fuji RDP*
Exposure:	*1 / 250 at F2.8*

Ice hockey brawl
PHOTOGRAPH BY RICK STEWART, PAGE 164
LA kings v Washington Capitals,
LA Forum, 1986

Camera:	*Canon T90 + strobes*
Lens:	*Canon 300mm F2.8 L*
Film:	*Fuji 100 RDP*
Exposure:	*1 / 250 at F4*

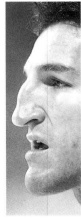

Tim Hunter
PHOTOGRAPH BY MIKE POWELL, PAGE 165
NHL Ice Hockey, LA Forum, 1991

Camera:	*Canon EOS 1*
	+ Stadium Strobe Lighting
Lens:	*Canon 80-200mm F2.8 L*
Film:	*Fuji 100 RDP*
Exposure:	*1 / 250 at F4.0*

Konishiki (The Dump Truck)
PHOTOGRAPH BY CHRIS COLE
PAGES 166 & 167
First Sumo Bashai Outside Japan,
Albert Hall, London, 1991

Camera:	*Canon EOS 1*
Lens:	*Canon EOS 400mm F2.8L*
	+ EOS 1.4 converter
Film:	*Kodak EPT*
Exposure:	*1 / 250 at F4*

Baja 1000
PHOTOGRAPH BY MIKE POWELL, PAGE 168
Baja California, Mexico, 1993

Camera:	*Canon EOS 1*
Lens:	*Canon 300mm F2.8 L*
Film:	*Fuji Velvia*
Exposure:	*1 / 500 at F5.6*

Carl Lewis
PHOTOGRAPH BY MIKE POWELL, PAGE 169
Carl Lewis Warms Down, LA Coliseum,
California, 1992

Camera:	*Canon EOS 1*
Lens:	*Canon EOS 600mm F4.0 L*
Film:	*Kodak Plus X*
Exposure:	*1 / 500 at F4.0*

Townley Grammar School for Girls

20054

18. DEC. 1995

Visions of Sport

The 140 photographs in this book have been chosen
from more than six million images in the Allsport library.
The photographs and their availability in all corners of the world
would not have been possible without the help of the following:
The Photographers, Picture Researchers, Darkroom Staff,
Picture Desk Operators, Accounts Staff, Clerical Staff
and everyone else in the Allsport offices at

ALLSPORT UK
3 Greenlea Park
Prince George's Road
London SW19 2JD

Tel: (081) 685 1010 • Fax: (081) 648 5240

ALLSPORT USA
Suite 300
320 Wilshire Boulevard
Santa Monica
CA 90401

Tel: (310) 395 2955 • Fax: (310) 394 6099

ALLSPORT NEW YORK
13B Gramercy Place
280 Park Avenue South
New York 10010

Tel: (212) 979 0903 • Fax: (212) 979 0460

and the international network of agencies
on all five continents.

Kensington West Productions Ltd
5 Cattle Market, Hexham
Northumberland NE46 1NJ

Tel: (0434) 609933 • Fax: (0434) 600066